Praise for *The I*

"A magical journey that leads one most profound way. Maura McC strong, delicate, with a river-like fl of wisdom, knowledge, education, and spiritual experience to arrive at a completely authentic place: the soul's ability to guide us in the human experience of life. As a reader, I was taken home to things I already knew and riveted by elements my heart needed to discover. Thank you, Maura, for finding your path and showing us the truth of our interconnectedness through trees and intuition."

> — Chloe Rachel Gallaway, Author of *The Soulful Child: Twelve Years in the Wilderness,* and Editor and Founder of the VOICES book series™

"If you're looking to cultivate a deep and enduring relationship with your intuition, then *The Inner Tree* is the book for you. It's a beautiful, rich, luxurious, and inspiring read that will help you understand what's in the way of connecting with your own natural 'psychic' skill and learn how to trust yourself back into a love affair with it. This is a rare book in this arena, one that looks at how body, mind, and spirit conspire to make you the wise person you already are. In these critical times, the world needs more of us to operate from our deep knowing, and this book shows us the way!"

> — Marguerite Rigoglioso, Ph.D., Founding Director of Seven Sisters Mystery School, and Author of *The Cult of Divine Birth in Ancient Greece and Virgin Mother Goddesses of Antiquity*

"*The Inner Tree* guides us to navigate to our deepest roots, where we can tap into intuition through a process the author calls Presence Awareness. Maura lights our path by sharing her knowledge and powerful examples from personal experiences. I have no doubt she will inspire others as she has inspired me."

> — Emily Rodavich, Author of *Mystical Interludes* and *Mystical Interludes II,* Collections of Her Own and Other Ordinary People's Mystical Experiences

THE INNER TREE

*Discovering the Roots of Your Intuition and
Overcoming Barriers to Mastering It*

THE INNER TREE

Discovering the Roots of Your Intuition and Overcoming Barriers to Mastering It

Maura McCarley Torkildson

Cover Art: Maura McCarley Torkildson · *Cover Design:* Rolf Busch
Interior Design: Penelope Love

Library of Congress Cataloging-in-Publication Data

McCarley Torkildson, Maura
The Inner Tree: Discovering the Roots of Your Intuition and
Overcoming Barriers to Mastering It

p. cm.
Paperback ISBN: 978-1-947708-14-3
Ebook ISBN: 978-1-947708-34-1
Library of Congress Control Number: 2018952695

10 9 8 7 6 5 4 3 2 1
First Edition, August 2018

 CITRINE PUBLISHING
Asheville, North Carolina, U.S.A.
(828) 585-7030
Publisher@CitrinePublishing.com
www.CitrinePublishing.com

*This book is dedicated to all people
who have struggled to trust themselves:*

*You are more powerful, more amazing
and wiser than you know.*

*What I wish for you is
for you to see yourself in all your glory.*

*What I hope for you is
total love and acceptance
of your humanity—all of it,
even the parts you
find hard to love!*

TABLE OF CONTENTS

FOREWORD

by Randy Fauver, Ph.D.

We humans are magnificent beyond our understanding. It is our birthright, our gift, and our responsibility to grow and blossom into ever-fuller expression of our magnificence. Intuition loves to help us along the way. Einstein famously said the most important question we have to answer for ourselves is whether or not we live in a friendly universe. When we open our hearts to the voice of intuition, we come to the realization that the universe supports our growth and courageous expression in every moment. We begin to welcome the creative connection between all things, inner and outer, and learn to trust ourselves and the healing wisdom that comes from within.

It is my great honor to write this Foreword to Maura Torkildson's book. She has created a masterful guide to developing our intuitive abilities. Building a relationship with our inner source of knowing is one of the most important and rewarding tasks we can undertake. By connecting with our intuition, we can experience a sense of safety and comfort in everyday life, we can discover an immediately responsive source of useful information that helps us make better decisions, and we can uncover a profound source of connection with the divine, the all-that-is which underlies and gives meaning to our lives.

In this foreword we will first consider some of the defining characteristics of intuition, and show some of the ways I've experienced these characteristics by sharing stories of how intuition has played a pivotal role in my life. Then we will look at some of the scientific evidence supporting Maura Torkildson's groundbreaking new model for how to develop your own intuition.

LESSONS ALONG THE WAY

Inner Life

One of the most important characteristics of intuition is that we have to become aware of our inner world, and especially of our emotions. I learned to positively engage with my inner experiences initially through psychotherapy, while living in beautiful Boulder, Colorado. After several years of digging through and clearing out the first masses of my collected dysfunctions and distortions, I began to realize a yearning for connection with something larger than myself. I joined a group of people who gathered weekly to sing and dance sacred songs from all the world's spiritual traditions. This opened me up to my spiritual nature, where I discovered connection with self, with others, and with the divine seems to occur through the heart. This was new to me. I sang and danced and continued therapy as I welcomed this budding awareness. I began to have more "synchronous" events occur, and I began to follow the first proddings of my budding intuition.

Signals

The signals of intuition come in many forms. Sometimes they appear as inner hints or voices, sometimes as outer signs or suggestions. Sometimes they come as the "still, small voice" of Christian traditions, other times as the more visceral urgings of a gut feeling. They may also rise into conscious awareness sourced in the unconscious mind. As I began to feel more comfortable in who I am, more whole, I also recognized a growing discomfort. The emotional work and spiritual worship began to feel stagnant, unrewarding. I cast about for insight as to what I should do. Then one day I received an unrequested brochure in the mail for Steamboat Springs, Colorado. The brochure's cover included a photo of a young boy sitting on a split-log fence with tall mountains behind him. I was doing inner child work at the time and this boy looked just like the child-me I'd been working with. The image rang something strong and true within me. I took it as a sign and, still with some doubts, prepared to move there.

Confirmation

Intuition doesn't explain or rationalize. This can be a helpful tool for discerning the difference between genuine intuition and what I call "head noise." In this case, I chose to accept the sense that I should move to Steamboat. I left my job, my friends, and my support community to go to a place where I didn't know anyone, for a reason I couldn't fully explain, even to myself.

When we choose to follow our intuitions, we will often receive immediate confirmation that we're on the right path. Rather than the familiar refrain of "one step forward, two steps back," when we move in alignment with our inner leadings we frequently discover that when we take one step forward, the universe takes two more steps forward on our behalf. As I crossed the final mountain pass that led to my new home, I felt an urge to drive my fully loaded car down a narrow dirt road going deeper into the tops of the mountains. I stopped in a high mountain meadow, walked to a small rock outcropping at its edge, and sat down. The meadow was filled with wildflowers, birds were singing, and the sun filled the air with an incredible glow. As I took it all in, allowing it to fill me, I felt an all-encompassing presence embrace me, holding me in an experience of pure love. Tears flowed down my face as I cried with relief, letting the love wash away all my fears. The problems I'd been working through in therapy seemed to dissolve into the soil of the field and I emerged a new person, clear, clean, and glowing, filled with a quiet joy and a confident knowing that I was in the right place. I spent many years in that town. Beautiful, rich years filled with love and growth and connection. And it all happened because I was willing to take a crazy chance, to listen to my intuition and to act on its completely non-rational guidance.

Action

And that's another principle of intuition. We need to act on it, with courage and confidence. I had recently received certification as a massage therapist and was doing part-time work for a massage center when I received clear intuitive guidance to open an alternative healing center. I had little experience with healing work and in no way felt ready to start my own private practice, let alone start up a group practice. Still, it was repeated guidance from my intuition, so my only decision was whether or not I'd have the courage to act. Fortunately, I chose yes.

I put an ad in the local paper (this was in the pre-Internet days) and within a week more than fifteen therapists responded. I set a date for us all to meet and discuss the business plan. When the day of the meeting finally arrived, I was as prepared as I could be. The people who showed up worked with a wide range of healing modalities, and every person there had far more experience than me. I answered their questions as best I could, but some of their questions seemed sharp and it felt like the meeting went horribly wrong. When it was over, not a single person had said they would sign up.

I was in shock. I mean, this is what guidance had told me to do, so why didn't it work? Whatever happened to "one step forward and the universe takes two more steps for you"?! I stewed in my confusion for three days, constantly praying and asking what I should do. Silence was the only response. Finally, I screwed up my courage and called one person from the meeting and asked if she would be willing to work together. Much to my surprise, she said yes. And so did the next person, and the next. By the end of the evening, ten therapists had agreed to join the group practice!

I turned again to prayer and asked, "Why didn't you tell me what to do these past three days?" The response was, "I already did. You just had to do it." That's when I learned that trusting intuition, and taking action based on that trust, strengthens our relationship with it, which leads to increasing clarity in receiving intuition's guidance.

The alternative healing center was an immediate hit in our small town. It grew rapidly to have offices in three towns across northern Colorado. Each office was associated with a conventional medical center, and we had an average of fifteen therapists offering more than thirty different healing modalities.

Synchronicity

Another expression of intuition is what Carl Jung called synchronicity, or a meaningful coincidence. While running the healing center, several people told me I should meet the spiritual leader of a local Native American community. I didn't have an easy way to reach him, and thought I was a bit too busy anyway, so I never took the initiative to follow up on their recommendations. I did, however, accept an invitation to take part in a sweat lodge hosted by a visiting Lakota ceremonial leader. During the hours of preparation for the sweat I started talking with a new person I'd met there. Our conversation deepened as we discovered shared beliefs, a shared sense of purpose, and shared understandings. After talking for about forty-five minutes, it became apparent to both of us that we had a lot of work to do together. That's when we introduced ourselves.

It turned out he was the spiritual leader/healer I'd been told to meet. He too had been told by several people over the course of several months that he should meet me; but in contrast to my attitude of passive neglect, he waited with confidence that we would meet when the time was right. When he was invited to take part in this sweat lodge ceremony outside his own community, he followed his inner knowing that he should attend. We spoke often after that initial meeting, then he took on the responsibility of training me and invited me into his community. I spent the next several years apprenticing with him and working with the people in his community.

Emotional Housekeeping

Early in my training, I learned that developing intuition calls for us to deal with and let go of our emotional baggage. My teacher said we can help others heal only to the degree that we ourselves have healed. That didn't make sense to my then-Western mindset. I thought medicines and treatments did the healing regardless of how much inner work the doctor or therapist had done. Oh how wrong I was. The first year or two we worked together was focused on healing me first. Under his guidance and with the help of spirit teachers, I worked through and released a host of old pains and distorted beliefs that had limited my ability to connect with spirit. Only after some of the larger impediments were resolved and removed could I see clearly enough that he let me work with others. Most psychotherapist training programs also require their students to go through therapy themselves. This clearing out of the old calls us to experience our stored emotional pain, grief, and sadness. As a result, we become better able to experience the full range of our own emotions and better able to read and be with the emotions of others.

Relationship

Increasing our emotional openness leads to a deepening of our relationships. This is another key principle of intuition. We can think of our intuition as an "other" with which we are developing a relationship. As we learn to trust and act on our intuitions, the intuitions become stronger and more frequent. We then develop a reciprocal relationship in which we can ask specific questions, or ask that the guidance be communicated in ways that are easier for us to understand.

When I was working with the Native American healer, he taught me how to talk with helping spirits and how to build relationships with them. Many Native American prayers include the phrase "all my relations." In this deeply relational experience of the world, plants, animals, and even places are seen as having their own forms of consciousness with which we humans can build relationships for the benefit of all.

In medicine and psychotherapy, the therapeutic relationship has been identified as a key component in the healing process. The quality of the therapeutic relationship plays a major role in how effective the treatment is. The dynamics of the healing ritual and the healing relationship are the same whether the treatment comes from a psychotherapist, a physician, or a Native American healer. You've probably heard that we first have to love ourselves before we can truly love another. The same principle applies here. The practices in this book will help you develop a therapeutic relationship with yourself, so you can then build a more solid and stable relationship with your intuition.

Spiritual Practice

Through the daily practice of relationship with intuition, I came to recognize that the world is alive with relationships and meaning. I came to understand that the world around us actively encourages our development as spiritual beings, and that we can learn to read these messages in the same way enlightened people of old were able to read the state of the world by observing a falling leaf. My world came alive with richness and understanding. When we acknowledge the depth of our interconnection with all things, our ordinary lives become extraordinary, and we see the world through new eyes. Every day becomes filled with miracles and magic. After years working with my physical and nonphysical teachers, engaging with them in healing practices for myself and others, I came to realize that every moment of our lives is filled with meaning and potential. Developing intuition is, in the end, a deeply spiritual practice; we come to realize that intuition, when accurately understood, is the voice for spirit.

Variations

These are some of the lessons I've learned about working with intuition. The principles listed above are neither prescriptive nor exhaustive, they are just some of the things I've learned along the way and presented in the order I experienced them. You will likely discover similar lessons in your own journey of working with intuition, and will probably also learn many others. Learning these lessons seems to be an iterative process. As I began to pay attention to my intuitive promptings, I got initial glimmers about most or even all of these lessons. Then as I continued to build a relationship with my intuition, I began to trust it more. As the relationship deepened and became stronger, intuition showed more of itself to me and I came to understand each of the lessons in a richer, more nuanced way. Around and around we go, in an ever-deepening spiral dance of discovery. I wish you a joy-filled dance as you build a relationship with your own intuition.

THE SCIENCE OF INTUITION

Changes

As I internalized the lessons learned through working in the Native community and the healing center, I saw that I was to embark on a new adventure, bringing these understandings into the world of academia. I returned to school at forty-one years old, leaving my business and community behind to learn the tools of science. I studied spirituality, psychology, and healing at some of the top schools in the country, including Harvard and Stanford universities, and found inspiring teachers, new ways of thinking, and dear friends along the way.

Following the universe's gentle guidance, I began doing research in Stanford University's School of Medicine. I relished this opportunity to stretch my wings in the field of medicine. While completing a dissertation study on the health benefits of a psycho-spiritual intervention for women with cancer, I also founded a research and education program at Stanford. The program was based on the principles I'd learned in the Native community—that consciousness precedes and gives rise to form—and was supported by the best-quality leading-edge scientific research. These were exciting times. What I had thought were radical ideas found broad support among the faculty, who recognized the need to bring more of who we are as people into the healing process. I've since left Stanford after completing my research there and now teach what I've learned about science, consciousness, and healing to the next generation of leaders who will move this work forward.

Science, Religion, and Consciousness

Both science and religion seek to help us understand who we are and the nature of the world around us. There is a surprising amount of agreement between the two. Science and religion don't have to be in conflict. Religions have been exploring these questions for many thousands of years, while Western science has sought answers to these questions for only a few hundred. The more science advances, the more congruent its findings are with the various religions. It's not that science and religion conflict with each other, it may be only that science is too young to understand.

As we turn our attention to the scientific evidence supporting intuition, we first have to consider the possibility that we live in a conscious universe, that everything we see, touch, smell, and experience is an expression of consciousness. This possibility is directly in line with the teachings of the major religions (Huxley 1945/2009), and is also consistent with the latest scientific findings.

Neils Bohr (1934), one of the founding developers of quantum theory, wrote that nothing can be said to exist except in relation to consciousness, and further that consciousness itself cannot be said to exist except as it relates to other consciousness. More modern theorists, like physicist David Bohm (1980), neurosurgeon Karl Pribram (Talbot 1991), and philosopher Christian de Quincy (2002), have suggested that the entire universe is made of mind stuff, that physical matter is a form of congealed consciousness. Physicist Sir James Jeans wrote (qtd. in Henry 2005):

> The stream of knowledge is heading toward a non-mechanical reality; the universe begins to look more like a great thought than like a great machine. Mind no longer appears to be an accidental intruder into the realm of matter . . . we ought rather hail it as the creator and governor of the realm of matter. (p. 29)

After decades of reviewing the research literature in the field of consciousness studies, eight leading scientists (Beauregard et al. 2014) wrote a paper calling for the development of a new science of consciousness to replace the limiting strictures of Western society's current, materialist model.

Eastern cultures in particular have rigorously and systematically explored the dimensions of consciousness for thousands of years. One English word for entering into heightened and expanded awareness of consciousness is enlightenment. The Buddha (Guatama Siddhartha) is said to have become enlightened after he sat beneath the Bodhi tree for seven days. Lao Tzu (*Laozi;* old master) is also said to have become enlightened while sitting beneath a tree, this time while watching a leaf lazily drift to the ground. Spending time with trees seems to awaken some primordial relationship between ourselves and pure consciousness; somewhere along that journey we open to intuition.

Communion with Trees and Nature

The founder of Western medicine, Hippocrates, is quoted as saying, "Nature itself is the best physician." Spending time with trees and opening to your intuition are integral parts of a Japanese practice called forest bathing (*shinrin-yoku*), which has been part of Japan's national health program since 1984. Forest bathing involves quietly relaxing under the trees or casually walking through them, which research has found to provide a wide range of health benefits (Lee et al. 2011, Park et al. 2009). When we exercise in nature we gain physical health benefits and increased vitality beyond what occurs during exercise in man-made environments (Ryan et al. 2010, Haluza, Schönbauer, and Cervinka 2014). Nature helps us think more clearly (Berman, Jonides, and Kaplan 2008) and more creatively (Atchley, Strayer, and Atchley 2012). Being in nature also improves our mood and positive emotions, while reducing stress and negative emotions (Marselle, Irvine, and Warber 2014).

The quality of our experiences in nature seems to matter at least as much as the quantity of time we spend there. Allowing ourselves to experience a sense of awe and wonder during our excursions into the natural world seems to increase the amount of benefit we receive (Sato and Conner 2013). Walking in nature confers physical, psychological, social, and spiritual benefits (Brymer, Cuddihy, and Sharma-Brymer 2010, Maller et al. 2006). Remember Buddha and Lao Tzu sitting under their trees? Many cultures use time alone in nature as a means for gaining insight, wisdom, and growth. Even Western research shows that spending time in nature tends to build our sense of connection with our spiritual selves and with the divine (Snell and Simmonds 2012). As we develop a sense of relatedness with nature, we take those benefits with us when we return to our human-built environments (Nisbet, Zelenski, and Murphy 2011, Talbot and Kaplan 1986).

When we walk through the woods, we join a community filled with lively and meaningful conversation. Little recognized outside the fields of biology and botany, trees form complex social structures using intricate and multilayered methods of communication (for a good summary, see Wohlleben 2016). The trees create social structures within each species and between species, sharing nutritional resources, messages about incoming plants and animals, and much, much more. The trees support each other in life, in death, and after death, all mediated through a range of communication channels. Trees talk with other plants as well, passing along messages to support the community, and trees and plants both talk with animals. Again, these types of communications between species are well documented in the scientific literature; it's not commonly known because we scientists haven't effectively shared these findings outside scientific circles.

Animals, too, talk with each other, and not just to say "Here is food," or "There's a threat." There is a vast body of research demonstrating that animals have emotions, inner lives, and social lives as richly varied as our own (see for example Wohlleben 2017, Montgomery 2015). Complex constructs of consciousness, what we experience as thoughts and emotions, appear to be common to all living beings. An international gathering of neuroscientists (Low et al. 2012) proclaimed the experience of consciousness and emotions is not limited to animals whose brain structures closely mimic our own.

Orcas (killer whales) discuss daily events and pass along learning from generation to generation. Linguists have recognized that different pods of orcas use different languages, not just variations on the same language (Ford 1991). Individual orcas and dolphins have unique names for themselves, use those names in communication with each other (King and Janik 2013), and communicate through a wide range of nonverbal signals as well (Pryor 1990). The evidence for primate self-awareness and symbolic communication is overwhelming, including their ability to communicate with other species in an intelligent manner (Savage-Rumbaugh, Mintz Fields, and

Taglialatela 2000). This is not surprising to most people, given that these species have highly developed brains. How then do we explain a grey parrot, with its much more primitive brain, who uses proper English words and rules of syntax to make accurate, specific, and appropriate statements that display self-awareness, emotions, and a highly developed consciousness (Pepperberg 2006, 2000)? Or an insect like the treehopper being able to tell its offspring some distance away what kind of predator is in the area (Cocroft 1999)? Even single-celled organisms appear to have complex communication systems allowing them to perform specialized duties in service to their larger community (Miller and Bassler 2001). "These and other findings have led to speculation that [bacteria share] a common 'language,' a bacterial Esperanto providing communication between species" (Bassler 2001, p. 17).

So far, however, we have only addressed purely mechanical means of plant and animal communication using chemical, physical, or sound signals. These communication methods could be relevant to the unconscious model of intuition in humans, but intuition is so much more. If we humans have access to information through non-ordinary means, we would expect to see examples of non-ordinary communication in plants and animals too.

Support for the existence of unifying fields of consciousness can be found in the biology and the study of animal behavior. You've probably seen how rapidly a flock of birds or a school of fish can change direction. These actions propagate through the group approximately three to five times faster than would be expected if the group's members were responding to visual stimuli. The flock or school performs turns and evasive maneuvers faster as a group than would be possible if each individual responded to the movements of a specific leader. The group displays this coherence even when the movement initiates at the rear of the group, unseen by the individuals at the front (Potts 1984). This suggests the existence of a group mind, or some other non-ordinary means of sharing information. Ant colonies and beehives also show group thinking, with each individual performing as if they were a single cell within a larger "super-organism" that itself displays evidence of unified consciousness and self-awareness, notably when the individuals are not able to use their ordinary means of communication (Hölldobler and Wilson 2009). Mound-building termites in Africa use a combination of chemical and visual signals to coordinate construction of towering colonies. Biologist Eugene Marais put a thick sheet of steel into one of these mounds, damaging the intricate network of pathways inside and effectively splitting the colony in two. With the steel sheet blocking the termites' ordinary means of communication, each group of termites rebuilt their mound separately. The resulting structures meshed perfectly with each other as if the steel plate wasn't there (Marais 1937).

We humans are part of this tapestry of life. In his biophilia hypothesis, biologist E. O. Wilson (1984) described our tendency to seek out and enjoy the world of plants, animals, and wilderness as a drive toward wholeness through building healthy relationships with the world around us. With all this communication going on within and between plant and animal species, is it really so hard to consider the possibility they might want to communicate with us as well? Indigenous cultures around the world have built healthy relationships with plants, animals, and landscapes; they tell us that nature yearns to talk with you as well.

To illustrate this possibility with another story from my own life, when I was considering which school to attend next I visited Bastyr University, perhaps the top natural medicine school in the country. Their beautiful campus is built around an old monastery just outside Seattle, in the middle of a heavily forested state park. I was excited about the school based on what I'd read, and even more so after talking with the people there. But coming fresh from my time in the native community I needed to receive direct confirmation from the spirit level as well. So I followed a trail into the surrounding woods, then wandered off the path until I felt called by a small circle of trees. I rested my hand against one of the trees, quieting myself and joining with the circle, then asked if this school was the right place for me. The trees replied very clearly, "We are here for people exactly like you." With tears streaming down my face in humble gratitude, I thanked them and went back inside the school to register.

Author Hermann Hesse called trees "the most penetrating of preachers." He wrote, "Trees are sanctuaries. Whoever knows how to speak to them, whoever knows how to listen to them, can learn the truth. They do not preach learning and precepts, they preach, undeterred by particulars, the ancient law of life" (Hesse 1984). These ancient laws are still active and available to us today (Ingerman and Wesselman 2010).

I spoke with the trees at Bastyr University using a form of shamanic communication. Shamanism provides a set of tools that can help us listen to the world around us. It has been practiced for at least thirty thousand years in every inhabited part of the world (Eliade 1951/1964). In the shamanic way of knowing, our inner and outer worlds are part of a single informational matrix. Shamanism tells us that everything is alive, that everything is conscious, and that we can tune our awareness to different aspects of consciousness just as we can tune a radio to different stations (Krippner 2000). Shamanic reports on the informational nature of reality are consistent with each other, regardless of the society or region they come from. As we will see in the next section, our bodies seem to be aware of this larger field of information even when our conscious minds are not.

Perception

Direct communication with plants and animals is one of many forms intuition can take. Our minds and bodies are incredibly sensitive receivers for intuitive information, but the question remains as to how we actually perceive and process that information. Some people argue that when we bypass the rational, linear thinking processes of our conscious minds, we can access more of the information that we've picked up and retained in our unconscious minds. Multiple studies have shown that rational thought works well enough for simple decisions, but when faced with more complex situations we consistently make better choices by relying on intuition (Salvi et al. 2016, Dijksterhuis et al. 2006). Many business leaders attribute their success to intuition, and the business community regularly studies how to make better use of intuition (Dane and Pratt 2007, Gigerenzer 2007, Gladwell 2005, Woiceshyn 2009).

Intuition in these settings is still limited to the conventional view of the mind, though, with the brain doing all the work. Research on business intuition defines it as "affectively charged judgments that arise through rapid, nonconscious, and holistic associations" (Dane and Pratt 2007, p. 33). But what of other, non-ordinary ways of receiving intuitive information?

The pineal gland. The pineal gland is a tiny, fluid-filled organ located in the center of the brain. It is not part of the brain however, being located beneath and between the two brain hemispheres. Named for its structural resemblance to a pinecone, the pineal gland has often been associated with the third eye. Cultures and traditions as diverse as Ancient Greece and Egypt, Islam, Hinduism, and Buddhism describe the pineal gland and its energy centers as the location for clear vision into the spiritual world, the source of insight and spiritual wisdom (Cardinali 2016). French mathematician and philosopher René Descartes called it the seat of the soul and the source of our thoughts (Lopez-Munoz and Alamo 2011). According to modern medicine, the pineal gland regulates our levels of consciousness through the production of melatonin. It manages our daily sleep/wake cycle based on light using a well-mapped neural pathway beginning with the eyes, through several parts of the brain, and then to the gland (Moore 1995).

Less often acknowledged is that the majority of the gland's body is formed of light sensitive cells called pinealocytes. These cells function similarly to the rods and cones in the retina of the eyes and are capable of detecting light in near-dark conditions (Vigh et al. 2002). The entrance to the third eye is commonly identified as being between and just above the eyes and proceeding to a brilliant source of light in the center of the skull. The skull in this area is comprised of the frontal bone. Curiously, this portion of the frontal bone is one of the few boney structures in the body that is translucent to light. Our anatomy allows light to pass through the area identified as the spiritual third eye, where it has nearly free passage through the sinus cavities and between the two brain hemispheres straight back to an organ designed to see light in darkness that happens to regulate consciousness. Conventional medicine has nothing to say on this coincidence.

The fluid inside the pineal gland contains two different types of microcrystals (Baconnier et al. 2002), one of which expands and contracts in response to sounds or electromagnetic fields, producing an electrical charge through the piezoelectric effect. This type of crystal action is used in modern technology to tune in to different radio stations. Further research might find a relationship between the pineal gland's piezoelectric effect and shamanic descriptions of tuning their awareness to different levels of consciousness. As well, the crystals inside the pineal gland can produce their own light (Sahai and Sahai 2013) through a process called piezoluminescence (Atari 1982). This is consistent with descriptions of the kundalini experience (Krishna 1995) and other descriptions of spiritual light. Keep in mind that the pineal gland, with all its possible spiritual connections with inner vision, is intricately connected with the rest of the body through hormonal, chemical, and neuronal signaling systems.

Heart. There are other organs with which we might perceive intuitive information as well. My spirit level teachers describe the heart as the connecting point between ourselves and others. Sri Ramana Maharshi said it this way, "The entire Universe is condensed in the body, and the entire body in the Heart. Thus the Heart is the nucleus of the Whole Universe." In the West we learn that our thoughts are located in our brains. While the brain plays a role in our thoughts, compelling scientific evidence suggests it may not be the only, or even the primary, organ of thought.

Neurologist Peter Lorber performed a systematic study of

the CAT scans of more than 600 people with hydrocephalus, an abnormal enlargement of the brain ventricles (Lewin 1980). Among the sixty people in the most severe category, that is, those in which ninety-five percent or more of the cranial cavity was filled with cerebrospinal fluid rather than brain matter, many were profoundly retarded yet half were of normal or high intelligence. One young college student with an IQ of 126 and a first-class honors degree in mathematics was found to have "virtually no brain" (p. 1233). The youth's CAT scan revealed only a one millimeter thick layer of brain cells lining the inside of his skull. All the rest of the space where the cortex of the brain normally resides was filled with cerebrospinal fluid. Other neurologists studying people with hydrocephaly found similar results (Berker et al. 1992). If, as seems reasonable based on these reports, the locus of consciousness, thinking, memory, and regulation of physical processes was not in the nonexistent brain of the hydrocephalic college student, then where could management of these functions reside?

Dr. Andrew Armour (1991), while performing some early mapping of the heart's neuronal system, discovered both afferent (receiving) and efferent (sending) neurons connecting the heart not just to the brain but also to the rest of the body. In fact, he found more signals travel from the heart to the brain than from the brain to the heart. In his reference book for clinical cardiologists (Armour and Ardell 1994), Armour described the heart's intrinsic neural system as the "heart brain." Working closely with Dr. Armour, technologist Rollin McCraty (qtd in Strubbe 2001) said:

> We observed the heart was acting as though it had a mind of its own and was profoundly affecting perception, intelligence and awareness. Our studies dovetail with other researchers doing related work that more than simply being a blood pump, the heart is a highly complex, self-organized sensory organ with its own functional, intrinsic brain. (p. 46)

Viewing the heart as capable of cognition is consistent with later discoveries of inter- and intraganglionic neurons forming nested communication loops within the intrinsic cardiac nervous system. Combined with the afferent and efferent communication neurons, these complex networks of neurons in the heart match the structures found in the brain that were identified by Merker (2007) as being necessary to support consciousness and cognition. Armour (1999) wrote the heart brain is able to "process information, learn, remember and produce feelings of the heart and then transmit information from one cell to another, including emotional information" (41).

Later experiments performed by McCraty, Atkinson, and Bradley (2004a, b) at the Institute of HeartMath suggest the heart may be involved in nonordinary perceptive abilities as well. They attached participants to EEGs and ECGs to measure electrical activity in the brain and the heart. As found in other research (Radin and Lobach 2007, Bierman and Scholte 2002), McCraty et al. recorded significant changes in participant brainwave activity immediately prior to presenting participants with emotionally triggering visual stimuli. When they reviewed the data, however, they found the heart reacted to the stimulus first and sent a signal to the brain. Only then did the brain show a response to the impending stimulus. The heart appeared to be the original organ of perception, able to scan and meaningfully interpret the immediate future, at least in this set of experiments. It may well be, as Antoine de Saint-Exupéry wrote (1944/1995), that "it is only with the heart that one can see rightly; what is essential is invisible to the eye" (82).

Gut. Yet a third possible location for intuitive perception is the enteric system, which includes the stomach, intestines, and other associated structures in the abdomen. Our language is filled with phrases like having a gut feeling about something, a gut wrenching experience, or not being able to stomach a situation. The enteric neuronal system contains sufficient mass and complexity, including the ganglionic structures mentioned earlier, to warrant being called the second brain (Gershon 1998) or, if the cardiac neuronal system is included, the third brain (Greenlaw and Ruggiero 2015). There are more receptors for the molecules of emotion (Pert 1999) in the third brain than anywhere else in the body (Pert et al. 1985). Activities in our enteric neuronal system directly influence our brain's cognitive processes, our emotional states, and our ability to make intuitive decisions (Mayer 2011). Research performed at the Institute of Noetic Sciences by Dean Radin and Marilyn Schlitz (2005) provides at least one example of how the belly's brain could aid in intuition. They placed pairs of people who were in a romantic relationship into separate rooms in separate buildings. When the researchers showed a series of emotionally charged photographs at random times to one partner, the other partner's gastric processes showed identifiable changes at those same random times.

The Western model of a brain in the head, another in the heart, and a third in the belly closely matches the Chinese Taoist and Buddhist model of three principal energy centers (Cleary 2009). The upper *dantian* (or *tan t'ien,* energy center) is associated with the third eye and the pineal gland. It is responsible for perceiving and processing the higher spiritual energies, the source of wisdom. The middle dantian is associated with the heart. It is viewed as a cradle for the soul, a mixing bowl for the earth energies below and the spiritual energies above. The lower dantian is associated with the lower abdomen. It is responsible for our connection with the physical and natural worlds around us, the source of our vitality. According to Taoist philosophy, these three dantians receive, process, store, and transmit information to and from the internal and external environments, and serve important regulatory functions for the whole body. It seems again that the more Western science matures, the more closely it aligns with the world's religions and wisdom traditions.

Whole bodymind. Finally, our entire body may serve as a kind of information processing center, capable of receiving, storing, and communicating what is currently called intuitive information. There is much we have yet to understand about how we collect and process information in the body. Emotions have been mapped onto different parts of the body in patterns that are consistent across cultures, suggesting a biological rather than cultural basis for emotions and the parts of the body they are associated with (Nummenmaa et al. 2014). Some kinds of memories can be stored and shared at the level of individual cells (Burrill and Silver 2010). There are numerous accounts of organ transplant recipients experiencing changes in their personality that coincide with the characteristics of the organ donor (Pearsall, Schwartz, and Russek 2000), and of having memories of the donor's life even though the medical system does not share such information with recipients (Sylvia and Novak 1997). Dr. Paul Pearsall published the stories of more than a hundred organ transplant recipients who remembered parts of the donors' lives (Pearsall 1998), including the case of an eight-year-old girl who received a heart from a ten-year-old girl who had been murdered. After the transplant, the eight-year-old girl began having nightmares of being chased through the woods and attacked. She described the location and appearance of the male attacker so accurately the police were able to identify and arrest him. His confession matched the young girl's description of the events exactly.

What gets lost in this reductionistic discussion of cells and organs though, is the realization that science has uncovered multiple interacting systems at the organismic, social, and global levels that have not yet translated into the models of human functioning used in medicine or presented to the general population. These larger and less known systems may play an important role in intuition. We are more than the sum of our parts.

Every living cell produces and emits coherent light, similar to a laser (Gurwitsch 1925). This light can be used to determine health or sickness (Ives et al. 2014), serves important communication and organismic regulatory functions (Popp 2008), and has been found to travel through the body using the same pathways identified as energy meridians in Traditional Chinese Medicine (van Wijk, van der Greef, and van Wijk 2010). The Sufi mystic Rumi wrote "Your body is woven from the light of Heaven." When we meditate, our bodies store more of this light in our cells (Van Wijk et al. 2006, Van Wijk, Ackerman, and Van Wijk 2005). Because these fields of light within us interact with the world around us (van Wijk, van Wijk, and Cifra 2007, Cifra et al. 2007), we realize they may form another means for sending and receiving intuitive information.

The entire body may act as a liquid crystal, with each part resonating to its own frequencies and responding to the vibrations of the world around it. When light interacts with water in and around our cells, it creates a fourth state or phase of water—a liquid crystalline state (Pollack 2013). This highly structured and ordered fourth state stores, conducts, and produces electromagnetic energy, serving as a kind of energy transformer between ourselves and the environment (Pollack 2015). This liquid crystal latticework vibrates with electromagnetic and quantum information sourced from within our bodies and from our environments (Oschman and Pressman 2014, Becker and Selden 1985). Our bodies are exquisitely sensitive to the physical, mental, emotional, and energetic worlds around us.

The word intuition comes from the Latin word *intuēri,* which means learning from within or looking within. Interoception is the formal word for the awareness of our internal bodily processes and experiences. As we increase our interoceptive abilities to know what's happening inside us, we increase awareness of our emotions (Barrett et al. 2004), our ability to process those emotions (Füstös et al. 2013), and our sensitivity to others as well (Terasawa et al. 2014, Fukushima, Terasawa, and Umeda 2011). Even our sense of self seems to be inextricably connected with our environment (Tsakiris 2017), so as we increase awareness of ourselves we increase awareness of our environment (Herbert, Pollatos, and Schandry 2007). Increasing our interoceptive capacity has been shown experimentally to directly affect the accuracy of our intuition (Dunn et al. 2010).

Our bodies form the common thread running through all the perceptual abilities described above and below. As already discussed, our bodies receive and respond to a vast array of signals. Our task in developing our intuitive abilities then becomes increasing our ability to become consciously aware of these signals and our body's responses to them. In order to do this most effectively, we have to be willing to experience everything we keep inside. Contrary to conventional wisdom, acknowledging our painful emotions and experiences actually helps us feel fewer negative emotions and feel them less strongly (Ford et al. 2017), and helps us feel more positive emotions (Troy et al. 2018, Gross and Levenson 1997). The research evidence is clear—accepting our negative emotions helps us experience more positive emotions, improves our relationship with our bodies, strengthens our connection with those around us, and increases our intuitive abilities.

Extraordinary perception. Intuition in the common understanding is perhaps most closely associated with extrasensory (beyond our usual five senses) perception. A discussion of the scientific literature showing the reality and accuracy of these non-ordinary ways of knowing is beyond the scope of this brief foreword; suffice to say that the science supporting psychic phenomena is rigorous, comprehensive, and conclusive. Scientists who discount the reality of psychic phenomena are either unfamiliar with the literature or have philosophical rather than scientific objections. The scientists working in the field of psychic research today have moved beyond simply proving its existence to studying instead its characteristics and underlying mechanisms. If you are interested in learning the science behind psychic phenomena, and if you've made it this far into the Foreword then it seems you are, I recommend three books on the subject. The most approachable science-based book showing the ubiquitous nature of consciousness and the ordinariness of psychic phenomena was written by Dean Radin, *Entangled Minds: Extrasensory Experiences in a Quantum Reality* (2006). For a more extensive examination of current scientific knowledge of psychic phenomena, along with recommendations for future research directions, I recommend Cardeña, Palmer, and Marcusson-Clavertz's, *Parapsychology, A Handbook for the 21st Century* (2015). Finally, the best sourcebook for applying these many kinds of experiences to your personal development and explorations in consciousness is Friedman and Hartelius's *The Wiley-Blackwell Handbook of Transpersonal Psychology* (2013).

The bottom line is we don't yet know how it is that when a friend of a friend of a friend, whom we may never have met, experiences joy in their life, our emotional state improves as well (Christakis and Fowler 2013). We don't yet know how it is that we can change the results of physical processes through the use of our intention alone, but that's what one of the top physics journals in the world tells us (Radin and Nelson 1989). We don't yet know how it is the we can know what is taking place in another part of the world without using our five physical senses, but the evidence is clear that we can (Schwartz 2014). What we do know is that none of these seemingly anomalous human abilities violate the laws of nature; instead, they point us toward existing laws of nature Western science has yet to discover. What we can say with certainty is that intuition in all its various forms seems to be an innate human capacity that can be developed. And that's what Maura Torkildson's *The Inner Tree* is about.

Conclusion

Einstein wrote, "The intuitive mind is a sacred gift, and the rational mind its faithful servant. We have created a society that honors the servant and has forgotten the gift." Our societal addiction to mechanistic technologies has overshadowed the much more important technologies of intuition, consciousness, and personal transformation. Just as there is a science to our machines, so too is there a science to intuition.

The science of intuition follows recognizable patterns yielding consistent results. We've described some of them here in the Foreword. In this book, Maura shares with us her powerful insights and understandings about intuition, sharing new yet ancient techniques for expanding our intuitive abilities. Most books on this topic take the reader through a series of relaxation exercises designed to quiet the mind so we can have greater access to intuitive information. While these practices can help, learning them first is putting the cart before the horse. What most other books fail to acknowledge is that we all hold a collection of distorted beliefs and difficult emotions that impede our ability to receive clear intuitive signals. In this book, Maura guides us through the process of first clearing away those impediments so we can then see more clearly and develop our skills more effectively. Science shows we already have these intuitive abilities. We just have to remove the stuff that gets in the way of us recognizing it. Once we remove the impediments to seeing clearly, our vision opens to the wonder and mystery in everyday life.

Exploring our stored and unexamined pain as a path to deepening our relationship with our intuition becomes a spiritual practice. According to the "Gospel of Thomas," from the *Nag Hammadi Library* discovered in 1945, Jesus said "If you bring forth what is within you, what you bring forth will save you; if you do not bring forth what is within you, what is within you will destroy you" (Logion 70). These statements apply equally to both the wounds we hold secret and the gifts we have to share.

Science leads us to understand the interrelatedness of our inner and outer phenomenal worlds, leaving us with the radical realization that all of life is a single concrescence, a unified whole whose vibrational nature permeates and underlies the entire physical universe. Ram Dass said, "Belief is in your head; faith is in your heart." Faith comes from acting as if, and allowing the resulting experiences to shape your understanding. All that science can do is strengthen your belief in the existence of intuition; Maura's book can lead you to directly experience the incredible power of intuition. That's the gift this book holds for you: the opportunity to discover and embrace your own intuition; to discover the richness, beauty, and magic that surrounds you in every moment; and to discover for yourself a positive answer to Einstein's question at the start of this Foreword of whether or not we live in a friendly universe.

Randy Fauver, Ph.D.
August 2018

PREFACE

I have spent a lifetime moving towards offering the wisdom shared in this book. There was a time in my life when I didn't think I was intuitive. While I was always fascinated with magic and the esoteric, I grew up the daughter of a scientist in a science university town, where belief in the esoteric was ridiculed. I was trained to look outside myself for truth and for an understanding of reality. My family regularly went to church, where I was encouraged to look outside myself for God too. Nowhere in my life was I ever urged to look *inside* myself for truth.

I am not an outlier. Looking outside ourselves for answers is typical of our culture. For over two thousand years Western culture has trained humans to look outside themselves and to rely on experts to explain our reality to us. Most churches demanded that people come to them for a relationship with God. In some periods, it was life-threatening to look inward for answers. Western history is full of stories about the danger of finding truths inside yourself, especially if those truths didn't agree with prevailing views. Authentic mystics were often persecuted in their own lifetime, only to become canonized posthumously (because wisdom cannot be suppressed for long). In Europe, women were burned at the stake by the thousands for independent thinking. I believe we still carry the cellular and psychic memory of the Inquisition in our bodies. Recent research at the University of Zurich and ETH Zurich has shown that ancestral traumas can be handed down to subsequent generations via DNA, and can cause increased sensitivity to conditions related to the original trauma.[1] This persecution is not just history. People in parts of the world today are still in mortal danger because of their alternative views and beliefs. Is it any wonder that we turn away from looking inside for our own truth?

It wasn't until I was twenty-seven, when my daughter was born, that I had my wake-up call. As I gazed into my beautiful baby daughter's face, I began to think about her future as a woman growing up in a patriarchal world. In that moment, I made a commitment to work for change. Soon after, I entered a Women's Spirituality Master's Program and began to seek answers about why women were subordinate and why my life felt so empty of wholeness and magic. How I felt inside was in deep contrast to the myths of my cultural indoctrination—that we live in the best time to be born, in the modern era with all its technology, longer life spans, the comforts of modern living, and progressive thought. As groundbreaking as the Women's Spirituality Program was, there was a way in which the Divine was still held on a conceptual level rather than an experiential one. Even so, I had some profound first-encounters while participating in this program, although I often didn't understand many of them until later.

It wasn't until after I graduated that I really began to look inward. It was a breakdown in my world that led me in this direction. That breakdown was painful, yet necessary for my growth. At the time, I had grand plans for what I was going to do with my degree, but I was up against a culture that was not ready for my passions. More significantly, my ego took over and tried to lead the way, and as a result, I lost my way. At the time, I

1 https://www.ethz.ch/en/news-and-events/eth-news/news/2014/04/
vererbte-traumata.html

didn't really understand how my intuition worked. I wanted to, but I also had a lot of fear, along with a desire for fame.

After graduation, I started a business selling my sacred artwork and creating personal shrines for clients out of gourds grown in my garden. Crafting the gourds was a time-consuming process, and I invested all of myself into shaping them. The gourds were created after listening to the life stories of my clients, and each gourd became a personal shrine—a reflection of who they were. The gourds were magical. My intuition came through in their creation, although I was not aware that I was using my intuition at the time. I called it creativity. Oftentimes, design elements I added came from a design problem I was solving, but ended up being deeply meaningful to the client. The interesting thing was that these elements were never part of any conversation I'd had with the client; they came in through the creative problem-solving process. When I handed over the gourds, my clients would often say to me, "I never told you about that. How did you know to include it?"

This was my first real understanding of how my intuition worked. I learned that it came through my creativity. As I listened deeply to my clients' stories, I picked up information behind the words they were using. But I was only a fledgling at this point. During this time, I was also struggling mightily against a tide of financial issues, and my business and projects were going nowhere. There was little financial return for all the time and energy I put into the gourds, even though the clients truly loved them. My business model was not sustainable, and I burned myself out. I had no idea how to run a business, which didn't help either. But throughout all of this, the main problem was my ego. While my intuition was present in the creative process, I was ignoring all the subtle internal signals that I was headed down the wrong path.

One day it all came crashing down in a moment of extreme disillusionment and disappointment. On that particular day, I had rented a booth at a festival in Sebastopol, California. On my way there, I was driving down Old Lakewood Road—a narrow, dangerous road between Vallejo and Petaluma, California. A truck rode my tail, too close for comfort. As I approached a tree, I noticed that several vultures were eating a dead deer on the side of the road. They scattered, and a vulture flew up and crashed into the grille of my truck before I had a chance to react. I wasn't able to stop to check the damage until I got into Petaluma (it was too dangerous to pull over and I was running late). I shook after the frightening encounter, and part of me knew it was a message. Determined, I forged ahead to the festival anyway. The grille of my truck was broken and so was my sense of equanimity.

At the festival, there were many admirers of my artwork, but I sold very few items. I left, heavy with disappointment and enveloped in gloom. I was in debt up to my ears. I felt totally burned out, and a sinking gut nagged me all the way home. When I finally pulled into my driveway, I sat in the truck, avoiding going into the house. At that moment, I wanted to turn around and drive away from my life. *I could just turn the ignition and drive into the hills and never turn back,* I thought. But instead, I got out of the truck and took a walk up to a favorite tree on top of a hill near my home. I stopped at the tree and placed my hands on its trunk in greeting, as I am accustomed to doing. Then I sat down on a bench nearby and finally released my tears. As the tears flowed, shudders of grief shook my shoulders and my belly began to melt. Normally, I am shy about crying in public, but I didn't care. The pain was too urgent. People walked by me, obviously discomfited by my lack of composure as evidenced by the way they turned their heads and pretended I wasn't there.

Eventually, the sobs subsided and I sat for a few more moments in stillness. I rose and said good-bye to the tree, then walked back down the hill to my house. Once there, I found myself still unable to go in and face my family. So instead, I sat on the deck on the side of our house and cried some more as I compared myself to all the other women in my life that appeared to be supported in living their dream. Suddenly angry, I shook my fist at the sky and asked God, "What's wrong with me? Why am I so unworthy?" I railed, "Why have you abandoned me?"

As soon as these last words were spoken, an epiphany broke free. I became aware that it was actually the other way around. God hadn't abandoned me, I had abandoned Her. I had not been listening to the Divine force at my center, being far too busy following the desires of my ego. I wanted to be famous, I wanted success, I wanted to be seen, but what I had failed to understand was that my life wasn't about my ego's plan for glory. There was a bigger plan for me that had nothing to do with my ego, and I had been totally ignoring all the signs along the way.

With this new awareness, I relaxed a little and walked toward our back yard to take in the magic of my garden. Once there, my cat Loki came over to sit near me. We sat in companionable silence. I looked over at him. Now aware, the grip of fear loosened from my epiphany, I could viscerally feel how totally present he was. His ears perked and swiveled, picking up all the sounds. I sensed him experiencing the gentle breeze as it ruffled his long fur. Riveted with awe at his presence, a question welled up from deep within me. *I wonder what it is like to be so totally present in each moment?* My entire being now exhilarated by this question, I felt a new beginning emerge. I heard a presence within, calling me.

Soon after my experience in the garden, I bought a *Parabola* magazine at the bookstore. This particular issue had an interview with a man named Peter Kingsley. The subject of the interview was presence, awareness, and service. Captivated by the article, I boldly sent him an email. To be honest, I thought perhaps an assistant would respond and that would be that. Much to my surprise, he responded himself and invited me to a gathering in San Rafael. I hadn't realized he lived so near to me. Of course I went. While at the gathering, I experienced the raw aliveness of being truly present. There was something about his presence that evoked more presence from within me. I found myself pulled toward him by my inner muse. I studied with him for several years. He pointed the way toward my inner world, helping me to learn to navigate there, and manage the ego. My work with him profoundly changed my life.

It's not that I don't struggle anymore. In fact, I actually struggle more—or so it seems because I am aware of the struggle. The inner spiritual path is not an easy one. There is an element of meeting greater and greater challenges along the way, and the ego fights a mighty battle to stay in control. But the moments of sheer presence and the magic are worth the trials that come with it. I am anchored in a way I wasn't before, and from this place I share practices that have helped and continue to help me come back into balance when I do the very human things that pull me out of balance and find I have again become embroiled in the struggle. That too is part of the path.

My deepest desire, guided by the Divine being that lives at the center of me, is to share my experience and the wisdom gained on my journey so that it supports you on this path if it calls to you. It is awareness that leads us toward growth from the unseen, underground seed into the magical trees that we were always meant to be. Welcome to *The Inner Tree*.

Maura Torkildson
Concord, California
August 2018

INTRODUCTION

What would it be like to understand and trust your intuition, to know that your inner guidance system will work for you consistently? What would it take for you to trust that guidance system implicitly? There are reasons why we are often disengaged from our inner guidance. These include how we have been culturally indoctrinated to look outside ourselves for answers, and how we aren't encouraged to use our intuitive muscles and our body as tools for awareness. When you cultivate something, first you need to learn what it is and how it works; then you begin to develop the skills, you test them out and eventually gain mastery around them. This is true for your intuition as well. The good news is that you already have what it takes inside you to tap into your intuitive abilities. It has always been there, waiting patiently for you to pay attention. This book is an offering to you to help you cultivate your intuition and master those skills. In it, I share practices to help you use and trust your inner guidance. I also offer guidance on how to cultivate inner awareness and navigate your inner world, but it is up to you to do the cultivating, to practice, and to develop a fulfilling relationship with your inner world.

Throughout these pages, I share a lot of my own stories to help illustrate insights. We are storytelling creatures, and story is one of the best ways for us to learn. Story has always worked better for me than a list of tips and how-to suggestions, so this book is largely not written that way, although you will find some exercises and experiential components, like the guided meditation that comes with this book.

The Importance of Confirmation

Confirmation also plays a role in our learning and mastery. The stories we share can serve as confirmation, and so can relationships with other explorers of the innerverse and other people in our lives. As humans, we are social beings, and a huge part of operating in this world is interacting with others who act as mirrors to reflect back to us who we are. As I am sure you are aware, some mirrors are clearer than others. In fact, certain people can be like the mirrors at a circus sideshow; what they reflect is distorted and sometimes even grotesque. It is such a gift when we run across a mirror where the image is vibrant and we can see ourselves in all our glory and all our grit.

I hope that somewhere, sometime in your life, you have received the gift of confirmation. I bring it up because it is important to acknowledge that we rarely achieve simple tasks, much less great things on our own. *No man is an island. It takes a village to raise a child.* We've all heard these sayings hundreds of times, but how often have you ever sat and contemplated the fact that you don't operate independently of the whole of life? You are not alone. If you wish to live a connected life, then it's up to you to find and develop relationships in your life with other explorers, especially those who can provide a clear mirror. You can use those relationships to build your confidence as you explore the concepts in this book. If it weren't for the people who provided gentle, empowering validation along my path, I don't know that I would have discovered the roots of my own intuition.

I applaud you for choosing this book and deciding to take this journey with me. That says a lot about your intent to deepen your relationship with your inner world and to take responsibility for your own growth. Awareness is the first step, and the fact that you have picked up this book means that you are already aware. If you have read even this far, then you are following your inner desire for more—something that the outer world cannot give you.

How to dive deep to discover the roots of our intuition while we find our worldly roles and self-identity connected to, if not defined by, a world of form? Mother Nature has an app for that.

Given that this particular book fell into your hands, it's safe to say you are drawn to trees, and I can certainly understand that. Trees have been calling to me all my life, and there is more to them than our culture admits in its materialistic worldviews and need for scientific data to prove the significance of the natural world. So often as children, we are trained to look outside ourselves for answers to what is meaningful. I want to suggest that what is meaningful needs no proof and lies within you, waiting for you to uncover it. The outer world provides confirmation for our inner state if we notice and it's important to develop a relationship with your inner world. Only you can know what is right for you, but the world will provide messages and synchronicities along the way to guide you.

How to Use This Book

Since this book is part of your outer world, and includes what I have learned on my path, I encourage you to take what resonates with you and leave the rest. Let your intuitive practice begin right here. Trust yourself and your judgment, but be careful that your inner critic isn't running the show. Approach the book with curiosity (one of the practices I highly recommend) and with an open mind. Then check in with your gut. In my coaching work, I don't do one-size-fits-all prescriptions. Everyone has their own path, and we can also learn from each other. Since this book has entered your world, I am part of your world, and there is a reason for that—whether it is to provide contrast or to provide guidance.

My hope is that this book will open your awareness to your own gifts and create the inspiration needed for you to deepen your relationship with those gifts, to trust that they are real, and begin to use them.

SECTION I

UNDERSTANDING INTUITION

CHAPTER ONE

TREE WISDOM

The seed it grows from is the unseen
Awareness is its trunk
Its inner hollows are the senses
Its branches are the great elements
The objects of perception are its buds

The Mahabharata

We are, in essence, trees. There is a reason why trees have inspired us over the ages. The way I see it, our consciousness is a tree. Our roots reach all the way to eternity and our branches to Heaven. Awareness is our trunk. This is our Inner Tree. And then there are the trees that appear to be on the outside of us. They provide the air we breathe and hold the earth together at our feet. They provide trunks for us to climb and branches upon which we can hang out and contemplate the world. Animals nest in them or seek shelter in them. They provide food for us, for insects, and for other animals. Can you imagine a world without trees? They remind us of who we really are. Without them, we would be totally lost.

Most cultures around the world have myths about trees. The Norse had Yggdrasil; the Hebrews the Tree of Life and the Tree of Knowledge. The Druids had a whole system of knowledge, healing, and magic built around trees. The word "druid" means "oak-knower." *Dru* means both truth and tree. The Hamadryads were tree nymphs in Greek mythology. Buddha achieved enlightenment under a fig tree, the Bodhi Tree. The people of Madagascar had the Ancestor Tree in the Baobab. The list of mythological trees goes on and on.

Personally, I am not surprised that Buddha achieved enlightenment while sitting under a tree. Trees speak to me. They whisper mysteries as I walk among them. They call to me to place my hands on them as I pass by. And yes, they induce me to hug them. I like to lay my whole body against a tree. I can sense the energetic heart of a tree by placing my palms on it and closing my eyes.

I love trees. I live in Northern California, and my favorite haunts are out among trees. My favorite trees are oaks. Their mastery of gravity astonishes me. I stand under them, looking up in wonder at their ability to stand at angles or to hold massive, heavy branches both vertically and horizontally to the earth for decades, even centuries. This is a truly magical feat in my eyes. California bay trees and redwood trees come in a close second to oaks on my list of favorites. Thickets of bay trees create a fragrant and shadowy cathedral. Groves of redwood trees create their own primeval habitat, which conjures images of fairies, gnomes, and dinosaurs. California buckeye trees inspired my first novel, *The Curious Magic of Buckeye Groves*.

Trees exist on a different time frame than us. I imagine that to some trees, we humans are quite ephemeral creatures, somewhat like gnats are to us. Trees feel timeless. What wisdom could be gained by pausing and stepping into their time frame? Tolkien alluded to this in *The Lord of the Rings* with the Ents, slow-moving friends of the trees who took their time deciding what to do. I feel that slowing of time when I touch trees. Some trees in particular evoke a deep sense of stillness.

Trees fill our mythology, our fairy tales, and our stories. The Tree of Life, or other forms of the World Tree, stand out. There are so many representations of a Tree of Life across so many cultures that you can't ignore the importance of trees to human consciousness. A tree is employed to illustrate the biological origins and evolution of life on our planet in our science. It is used to explain the branches of our human families, and as a structure for charts and organization. I've seen pictures of placentas that look like trees. Our human nervous and vascular systems have branches like trees. Trees are fractal; their geometry is fractal, branching like so much of nature, so they embody reality on a deep level. Trees are clearly embedded in our psyche. The shape of a tree, with outreaching branches at the top and roots at the bottom, follows the shape of the Torus, which some physicists, like Nasseim Haramein, say is the shape of our Universe.

The three most well-known Western religions—Judaism, Christianity, and Islam—all have roots from early cultures in the Middle East, and the Tree of Life is central to all. It is a central part of the story of the birth of humanity and the earth. From Genesis, the story goes that the Tree of Life was placed in the center of the Garden of Eden along with the Tree of Knowledge of Good and Evil. In the story, after Adam and Eve ate the fruit from the Tree of Knowledge and were kicked out of the garden, the Tree of Life was guarded by cherubim. The quest we must embark upon is to regain entry to the garden again. It lives inside of us, and this part of the quest requires that we go inward. To taste of the fruit of inner knowing, we must first pass the cherubim, facing our fears and leaving our egos behind. That is the price of re-entry into the garden. There we will find our magic again. But of course, with great magic comes great responsibility. It cannot be done without taking responsibility for ourselves. This is not a quest we can ask others to do for us.

The Tree of Life is the central mystical symbol for the Kabbalah and represents Creation. I am not a student of the Kabbalah, but it feels aligned with the tree as consciousness (creation comes from consciousness rather than the other way around). Trees are also prominent in another myth of the "fall," which we will explore in more depth the next section on Inanna and the Huluppu Tree. There are so many reasons why trees are important to humans and I have barely scratched the surface with the examples I covered in this section.

Inanna and the Huluppu Tree

Some myths use trees to tell a story about our sense of separation from the magic of our Inner Tree and its connection to nature. One such myth comes from Sumeria, the myth about the Huluppu Tree. This story is about the destruction and domestication of trees—a sad preview of the wholesale destruction of forests by humanity in the modern world as well as our disconnection from our wild inner nature. The Goddess Inanna rescues a tree from the waters of the Euphrates. The tree had become unmoored after the initial act of creation, in which everything needed was brought into being, and the earth, heavens, and underworld had been separated. Inanna plants the Huluppu Tree in her holy garden. A snake, the Anzu bird, and the demon Lilith take up residence in the tree and Inanna laments. Desperate to remove the unwelcome guests, Inanna calls on her brother Utu to help her. He refuses. Next she calls on the warrior Gilgamesh. He agrees and rids the tree of the unwanted residents, after which he chops down the Huluppu Tree and makes a throne and a bed for Inanna out of the wood. In return, she uses parts of the tree to make implements of power, which she hands over to her brother and Gilgamesh.

I feel sorrow when I read this myth, because I believe it records man's burgeoning desire for dominance over our wild nature. The need for dominance and control is driven by the ego's fears around losing its constructed identity of self. This comes from socialization. Belonging in a patriarchal culture is contingent upon molding oneself to fit into the story our culture creates about reality and what it means to be human. In patriarchy, that story plays out against our wild nature. I see the ego as a safety mechanism in our predominantly fear-based society. Its role is to protect our social status and belonging. This is part of our makeup as social animals. The ego is there to help us navigate this surface of reality where we enter at our birth into a body. When we merge back into Unity, our separate identity dissolves into the wholeness of our soul. This happens at death, but can also happen before we die. Many rituals of the ancient world were about moving through that experience of identity death for spiritual growth. For a large part, we have lost those rituals in the modern world, and so have lost some wisdom. Our cultural story tells us that we are separate and individual beings, framing death as a tragedy. Death and grief are avoided and that leads us to desire a kind of permanence in that state—a state of material immortality. Of the numerous movies and cultural stories that deal with immortality, typically they are of a tragic nature (think vampires), which shows us that at least we are aware of the impact of that constant sense of separation. The ego will never have immortality; only the soul is eternal and the soul is immersed in Unity. Nothing can be separate from the whole of creation. That doesn't stop the ego from trying, even though it never could be in control in the first place. This is the primary conundrum of the ego. And yet, even the ego has its purpose, and perhaps compassion is the highest gift we can bring to it.

Later in this book we will look more closely at the ego, both to look at how it is an integral part of being human and to help you understand how it can pose a challenge to your intuitive abilities. You'll learn how to work with that.

In the myth about the Huluppu Tree, Inanna laments her wild nature in her tree, and when the tree is chopped down, her power is conceded to the patriarchal masculine. The power left to her is the power of her bed, where she will join with the masculine. Her deeper sexual nature flees to the desert with Lilith, the archetypal witch, where it will be preserved until she is ready to claim it again. Lilith will not and cannot be controlled, and yet until women embrace her, we will not be whole.

Being the Tree You Are: A Meditation
to Deepen Your Conscious Awareness

Find a place where you are comfortable and relaxed. Close your eyes and sink into yourself. Drop into that dark space inside where your awareness exists. Explore your awareness. You may find it has a texture, a substance. Normally, we feel substance with our skin, specifically our fingers. If we run our fingers across a surface, we feel the texture—smooth or bumpy or any number of things. Your inner landscape has texture that we only know through some internal sense. This is your trunk, the place where your senses come together in such a way to the Self that is aware. Now, stay present with that trunk and become aware of your root. This root goes so deep, it may feel endless. It goes down into the unknown. Can you sense the depth, and be aware of your origin in a place so deep it is a mystery? This is the unseen home of the seed of your being.

Now bring your awareness to your body, your limbs, and your skin. This is the place where you interact with the outside world, where you begin to have a separate sense of self; it is the place where you make a distinction between the inner you and the outer world around you. If you stay with this awareness of your limbs and your skin, notice how they are not disconnected from your trunk or your root. They are extensions of that trunk. Now you can become aware that what you think is "out there" is really part of you too, because it is all part of your experience, which happens inside you. You are completely incapable of stepping outside of yourself, as you experience the whole at all times, even when you are unaware of it. What is created "out there" is only the sense's projection of your inner experience. This is what I call "the surface of being." We are a great tree and our branches reach up, out, and down around us, creating the surface of our awareness, the mind, where we spend most of our attention and focus. The Vedics envisioned the mind as just another sense—a very different and wiser view than how Western culture conceives of the mind, as primary. That idea has not served us well.

Because the ego is a creature of the surface, and it is on constant alert for danger to its identity construct, it is mostly unaware of your trunk or home, or the seat of your awareness. The ego can trap you into the deception of "out there," but remember, being so trapped can keep you disengaged from your roots. To become aligned with your intuition, you must pay attention to your trunk and cultivate an awareness of the unseen realm of your roots. Remember that intuition is not something that comes to us from the outside, because there is no "outside." Intuition arises from the deepest part of us, where our roots meet eternity, the origin of our being, and the home of the Divine source of everything. Here, nothing ever changes; it is the heart of stillness and of infinite peace and love.

You are God experiencing Being. When the ego creates the experience of separation, we forget that we are Being, God. Unity is possible in every moment because it always is. In the quote from the Mahabharata that starts this chapter, it says: "*The objects of perception are its buds.*" Our perception shows us that life is constant change, and change implies movement. The truth is that the only thing that ever moves is our perception. How do I know this? It is a knowing I experience from being internally aligned with my trunk and my root. Do I experience this at all times? I do not. But the taste of that experience lingers and acts as a reminder to be aware. Standing in these human shoes, I experience the ego as the sense of separation every day of my life. Many times, this deception tricks me into forgetfulness. Only by remembering to be aware and present do I gain some small bit of mastery over this ephemeral ego trickster, and in doing so, I stay more aligned.

When you begin to open your awareness to your trunk and become aligned, you will soon realize that your trunk is a vast, endless universe. The navigation skills here are different than the ones we learned to use on the "outside." In our life, we may be graced with guides, as I was with Peter Kingsley, to point us inward. Ultimately, experience is our best teacher as we explore and learn to navigate the interior. Our experience, particularly our inner experience, is not always amenable to words. It is ineffable. As soon as we try to describe it, we are wrapping the mind/ego around an indescribable experience in an attempt to gain control (the ego desires what it cannot have), and the awareness drifts away from us. Talking about our experience, particularly speaking too soon, can disrupt our open awareness. I won't say that talking about the experience is wrong (no right or wrong here), but I do caution you to take care. The mind and the ego have a purpose too; they are the construct or vehicle in which we appear to move around on the surface of Being. Our spirit longs for our home. My being can feel the depth of my roots, but the home of my root is a mystery. It is a place my mind cannot reach, because the mind only exists on the tips of the branches. The home of my roots is veiled. All I can do is stay in touch with my longing, experience the profundity of my soul, and feel the love that reaches to meet me from there. It is helpful to stay in touch with your own longing while seeking to be aware of the ego's machinations. From there, your wisdom will grow.

We are using words here, metaphors really, to draw your awareness to your inner world and the Tree of Life. Ultimately, what matters most is experience, which is far more potent than belief. We pay so little attention to our experience, especially our inner experience. We deny it. We minimize it by calling it "imagination"—something that isn't quite real. We seek proof or confirmation for everything in the outer world (whether via science, religion, or the pursuit of status) and split reality into real and not quite real. How can that be so? We cannot split reality apart. There will never be proof for our inner reality. Our organs, our cells, our brain, and our DNA are not our inner world and will never adequately explain consciousness—this forgotten, unnamable, indefinable presence remains hidden from our awareness as we go about our distracted lives.

In my experience, after working with intuition for so many years, I have come to realize that our lives are a movement between the outer and the inner, the mind and Being. I have learned not to judge that. Judgment is a trap. It holds us hostage to an idea of perfection that is static and dense.

To use another metaphor, on this path we walk with one foot in each world, and that is how the unseen seed of our being grows into the tree that it is becoming. Come. Begin to navigate your inner world and watch your relationship with your intuition grow.

Beginning to Understand Your Inner World

I too have been on a long journey to begin to understand how to navigate my inner world and use my intuition, which is the fruit of the inner roots. In Western culture, intuition is not acknowledged as a viable source of information, although that is changing. At one time it was dangerous to use the intuitive arts, as they were seen as heresy; and in the scientific age, using the intuitive arts often includes being ridiculed and subjected to the rules of "proof."[2] Unless we grew up in a family that cultivated intuition, we likely didn't receive support for it, or it was actively repressed. It is becoming more accepted now; however, since in many ways it is not fully understood, we still do not learn how to cultivate it. Some people figure it out on their own, or they have someone in their life who acknowledges it or teaches them ways to navigate. I find that people often have a Hollywood view of the intuitive arts. Intuition, although it may appear to some like fireworks, often is much more subtle. In my experience, it is both much more subtle than it is shown on TV or in the movies, and also completely magical. It gets louder and more persistent the more we cultivate a *relationship* with it (and I use relationship here specifically because it is not an object or even a skill).

With intuition, the secret is first to notice it; second, to trust it is real; and third, to take the risk of acting on it (which deepens your trust). I use the word *trust* instead of *belief*

---

2 Proof is important in a court of law, medicine, and areas where there is great impact on others, and can be helpful for some important decisions. I am not arguing that proof is not important here, rather that when it comes to the meaning we derive from our inner experience, there is no need for it. Some things cannot be proven.

because I think trust goes deeper. Trust implies a form of surrender, which is what the ego must do. One must also start with an open mind. It helps to set aside right or wrong and take on an attitude of learning and experimentation. Keep in mind that our minds are built to look for patterns, and we often pay attention to the patterns that verify our current perception of the world, and ignore the rest. We are also very persuaded by our past. The past can be one of the most persuasive features of our lives. However, even the past is a story we create about it, according to the patterns of our habitual mind, and that story also morphs over time.

Our senses are a great gift, able to pick up so much, but we give attention to those things that validate our world view and ignore the rest. Fear and ego play a major role in this. Cultivating your intuition requires curiosity, openness, and courage. It requires leaving behind our preconceived ideas about our intuition, because we may only notice what validates that preconceived idea and ignore the rest. Dogma has no place in this equation. I have noticed how the human mind works to fit an experience into the prevailing dogma of whichever tradition we follow. Dogma can represent some part of truth, but the question is, what do we miss or override when we work so hard to adhere to dogma rather than being open to our experience as it evolves? Sometimes it can be helpful not to "make" meaning out of our experience too soon. When we do so, we kill the tender shoot that needs to remain under the surface for a while before it reaches the light. I know, I have done it often, giving in to my impatience. Who knows how many insights I have killed before they were allowed to emerge on their own?

The Unseen Seed in the Mahabharata quote is a mystery. We will never be able to fully penetrate this mystery with the mind, and it will always remain veiled, even as we grow in our understanding. Just like a seed that sprouts from the ground, the shape of the future tree is unknown. We may label the tree as a certain species, but even that limits our ability to receive the tree as it is. Our language and our words shape our perception.

What pops into your mind when you hear the word *tree?* I will guess that you get an image of a tree. What shape does that tree take in your mind's eye? Begin to examine what you see. Can you determine where that image came from? Sometimes the images that come with our words (labels) prevent us from seeing what is actually there. Likewise, intuition can be turned into language, but the language will never capture the whole of it as intuition is a pre-language resource.

There has been much discussion about intuition as a function of the right brain. There is also a "gut" truth to the origin of intuition in the gut due to the fact that we have almost as many neural networks in our gut as we do in our brain. The heart is involved here too, due to all the neural networks there—all are connected to the vagus nerve, which is also responsible for our social engagement system in our faces, eyes, and ears. In my experience, our bodies—nerves, vessels, muscles, organs, et al.—are only the surface of our being. Our bodies are our vehicle for navigating through this surface world. But reality goes much deeper than the world of form that we move around in. Intuition's origin is in the roots, and it is also embedded in our bodies through neural networks. Yet our experience can never be reduced down to neurons and physical functions. The vehicle is not the driver. There is a whole universe inside you. You will find it if you start to explore your inner world and the seat of your awareness, which is deeper than your gut, your nerves, and your body. It is connected to your body, but your body is not all of you. There is a subtle distinction here. I am not alluding to transcendence, something outside of us, but to what I might call *inscendance,* consciousness itself. It is not an "out of body" experience. My experience of this kind of language is misleading and part of what led to my confusion about my intuition.

You always have access to your inner world and the access point is where the roots of sensation come together. Sensation allows you to be aware. As with the Tree of Life, our inner roots go all the way to eternity. Don't just take my word for it, however. Set an intention to explore your inner world and begin to confirm your experience with your awareness and trust, and then see if what I am saying makes sense to you. At its heart, the universe is still—motionless. I think the only thing that ever moves is our perception, and we are as firmly rooted in reality as a tree is rooted in the earth.

A Word About Grounding

Many of the rituals and workshops I have attended started with grounding, and I have often seen the leaders use the metaphor of the tree to help people imagine that they have a root that goes to the core of the earth. These grounding exercises work because they allude to the tree we are, and help us become centered and aware. In my experience, grounding became much more powerful when I experienced it connecting to eternity inside myself, rather than imagining a root connecting somewhere outside of me. Peter used to tell me that is where True Earth is. You are always grounded. You may not be aware of it, and might feel unhinged, but the secret is to become aware of your grounding. The purpose of a grounding exercise is to bring your awareness to your groundedness. Our perception can become quite unanchored, seemingly floating and flitting around when we cede control to our minds. But remember, the mind is a creature of the tips of our branches, is enamored with form, and cannot fathom what lies at our roots. It is important for us to begin to journey inward and become aware of those roots. In fact, it will change your life if you stay attuned. Awareness is vital, and I remind you of that throughout this book, because it truly is the key. So simple, but so true.

So, how does one learn to trust the legitimacy of intuition and the inner world? We do so by attuning to our experience and accepting it without manufacturing meaning. By seeking linear explanations and attaching meaning too quickly, we may end up meddling with the process and ignoring the more subtle aspects. Describing what you experience can be helpful, but be aware that words are limiting. *The problem with words is that they are not the experience.* Try describing your experience of taste. You may find many words to describe the sensation, but you can never totally capture your experience with words alone, which is why the best way to communicate taste is to share food. With that said, it does hone our ability to become more precise about describing our felt sense[3] because it hones our attention. One way to increase your skill is to become much more aware of your body and all its subtle and overt sensations (about which I will go into in detail later). I see the body as your instrument of navigation. But, there inside of you, your universe is much more than the body. The body is the surface creature of your universe.

Presence is the Key

I began to give my inner world much more weight after I met Peter Kingsley. I remember the first time I went to hear him speak at an event in San Rafael. I went by myself—a courageous act for me back then. I was nervous about meeting him and about showing up in a community where I was a stranger. Somewhere inside me I already knew he would change my life and also call my ego to the carpet. I also didn't want the distraction or safety of a companion. I was committed and curious, so I went alone. When I entered the venue, I noticed rows of chairs lined up in a beautiful room; a series of large, paned windows spanned floor to ceiling; and the room had a beautiful wood floor. At the front of the room, red ornate cushions were scattered on the floor. The pillows and decor had a distinct Arabic flair. I sat in a chair behind the cushions, right next to one of the windows. People continued to enter and fill the seats. Some sat quietly conversing with each other

---

3 The *felt sense* is the embodiment (bringing awareness inside the body) of one's ever-changing sensory/energetic/emotional landscape. The *felt sense* moves our focus from actions and things happening outside us in the world to qualities of our present, internal experience (e.g. textures, colors, sensations). See Peter Levine's *Waking The Tiger: Healing Trauma* (North Atlantic Books, 1997) for more on *felt sense.*

as we waited for Peter to come out. Most people were sitting silently, waiting. It was a subdued but pregnant atmosphere. I would guess that there were about fifty people in the room. After waiting for about twenty minutes, Peter finally came into the room and sat in a large cushioned chair that had been placed for him front and center. A small table with a glass of water on it sat next to his chair. He situated himself in his chair, then silently gazed around the room at all the people. After moments of this, he made a quiet joke and laughed softly. At first his presence was understated and I thought, *What an odd sort of man.* Then he wove his spoken magic. As he spoke, I became more and more riveted to my chair. This man had a presence the likes of which I had never experienced before. And in his presence, I was also more present than I had ever been in my life. I don't even remember the topic of his talk now. What I do remember is the aliveness that swelled through me, which I had only experienced before in fleeting moments.

At one point he began to talk about our presence, here in the now, suggesting that there was nothing beyond what we were experiencing with our sensation in this moment. He spoke of the birds singing outside the window, the sunlight streaming in, the colors, shapes, and the taste of our awareness together there. As he spoke, my awareness deepened, expanded, and filled me. He looked out the window, gesturing and speaking to the wind in the trees, and said that our view from our seats, looking out on the world was the entirety of our present reality. He said reality went as far as our senses could take us, but that there was nothing beyond that which was inside our senses. We could believe many things, but there was no way to verify that anything existed outside of us. This was the first time I had heard anything like this in my life, and it rocked my world. He brought everyone in the room present by being so fully present himself. It was magic. Aware, present, alive ... are all words that attempt to capture my first and almost every other experience with him. However, the best word I can come up with is real— and even that one falls short.

This was the beginning of my journey into the tradition that

Peter carried—a tradition that traversed the roots of Western culture, Greek shamanism, Hermeticism and wound its way into Sufism, Jewish and Christian Mysticism, and into our own time through him (and others). This tradition always moves on when dogma takes over, as it always will. It is a mystical bird that flies where it will, cannot be captured, cannot be imprisoned by the fabric of our minds, only recognized by our spirit, which longs for it always. Peter opened doors for me into the Tree of Life, the Tree of Being. This presence is the key to your intuition, to knowing (as opposed to knowledge), to wisdom, and to becoming human. It is access to the divine source of life. It doesn't belong to us, it moves through us.

One other piece that Peter helped me understand is that we are only seeds; we haven't quite flowered into our full potential because we have yet to learn how to use our senses rather than being led around by them. I have alluded to this several times already when likening our current state of human being to that of "seeds" and "shoots" in our tree metaphor. Peter often spoke of the original meaning of *common sense*—using our senses to be present, aware, and to navigate. This, he said, was the original meaning of that phrase. He once stated that Aristotle, in the arrogance of his mind, never understood common sense. He alluded to the fact that our growth as humans had been arrested by Athenian philosophy, bastardizing and leaving behind the shamanic roots of the West and confusing the true foundations of our heritage.

As I sat there and listened to all of this, I didn't understand most of it, but a part of me knew he was speaking truth. It was my first taste of trusting my experience, and it wasn't a mental thing. Presence awareness rose from deep within me, and it changed my life. I am not the same person I was when I went to that meeting that day, or after working with Peter for several years afterward.

All that I have written here is just a map. It may point the way, but the rest is up to you. Allow yourself to become truly present with all your sensation. Surrender yourself to it, and all that mental chatter goes away, like fog clearing in the sunlight, allowing you to finally see your surroundings, to feel warmth on your face and body, and to emerge from the illusions of the mind. Your mind will come back; it is part of the fabric of reality too.

The mind won't like this exercise because it cannot exist in the same place as your Presence. Pema Chodron calls this Natural Awareness and training the mind. Whichever tradition introduces you to this way, when you become present, you begin to allow the divine source that lives in the deepest part of you to come to light and move through you, guiding and informing you. This allows you to tap into the source of your intuition.

You can find my Presence Awareness Meditation audio at http://www.mauratorkildsoncoaching.com. The meditation is intended to bring you present, to give you a taste. It is up to you to find your way. Remember to do it on your own, as often as you can remember. Don't become conditioned to listen to my audio, as it is only there to open the door to your own awareness. I can't take you to where you need to go. You have to allow that for yourself. If you don't have my audio, or a way to listen, then read the following and see if you can find your own way into presence starting here. Use the following instructions as a guide, but be aware of what is present for you rather than my examples. Read it through first to get a feel for the way in, then surrender into the now.

Wherever you are...

To relax, bring your awareness to your breath.

Breathing in again, notice where there may be tension in your body.

As you exhale, allow your body to relax.

Now, expand your awareness to all that is present in your sensation.

Open your hearing to the sound of all that is present to your ears—the air system, the traffic, the murmur of voices, the shuffling of chairs, etc.

Now open further; notice the felt sensations, like a tingle on the tip of your nose, the tips of your fingers...

Now, as you hold these in your awareness, expand your awareness to notice the pressure of your seat in the chair, your feet on the ground...

Notice the feel of your hair as it touches your neck, face...

Continue to open your awareness to all that is present.

You may find yourself opening to what is inside you as well, noticing how all your sensation comes together inside you and that it has substance.

You may become aware of stillness.

Just stay with it as long as you can, letting go, being aware...

Notice when your mind intrudes and then let go again...

And follow your longing...

Building awareness gives us access to our ethereal body, or what I like to think of as "the spirit body" that dwells inside this shell that is the outer body. When I open my awareness to all that is present around me, I become present to my inner world as well. The inner world operates differently than the outer, and the inner world is even more rich and amazing and vast. We carry a whole universe around inside us—I call it the *innerverse*. I am not referring to guts and organs; I'm talking about the dark place inside us that houses our spirit, our life— the part of us that is having the experience. It is rare that we pay attention to this vast innerverse or give it credence, as we are conditioned to be mesmerized by our chattering minds and enchanted by the world of form. Peter used to say that deception was built into reality. The world of form is that deception, and the ego the unwitting agent of that deception.

Being aware through the bodily sensations builds your in-tuitive muscles. In my own life, I learned this practice through my studies with my spiritual mentor. Under his guidance, I became aware of a powerful intuitive capacity that has served me well and supports my self-understanding as well as my work with others. Practice presence awareness whenever you can re-member to do so. It is the doorway to your intuition's true roots.

Beginning to Navigate

I have suggested that becoming aware and present as the key to developing your intuition. I have also suggested that there is a natural movement, in and out of awareness, from the mind to presence and back again. Navigating the tides of our being and understanding our intuition requires some skill, and much like anything else, what we pay attention to and practice increases. I have found that emotions, attachments, and fears can get in the way of understanding and using intuition. These are the things we must learn to master in order to strengthen our intuitive muscles. It helps to do emotional healing and to develop emotional intelligence. The more aware you are of your emotions and how to process them, the more you will develop confidence in yourself and your ability to navigate your life. The more aware you are of your fears and how to work with them, the more you become resilient. These both lead to trust; trust in your ability to overcome, to heal, to persevere, and to listen to your inner guidance. For that reason, I have included sections in this book on dealing with emotions and fear, and how they show up in your body.

Your body is a sacred tool of awareness and is the gift that the universe gave you in which to house your spirit. Understanding how it works is part of your sacred task in this lifetime. The body has been denigrated and marginalized over the course of Western history, but the tide is changing. Much of the trajectory of Western spirituality has been toward transcendence. Transcendence is defined as existence or experience beyond the normal or physical level. But we misunderstand that to mean escaping the body by floating out of it, or something similar (for example, astral travel). But all of that happens inside our sensation and awareness, which exist more below the surface (where our awareness typically is) rather than outside it. We can never go outside ourselves (a truth which is really the ultimate in logic). *We are always inside our awareness.* But conceptually, we think of transcendence as leaving the body, and hold our minds up on a pedestal, pretending they are somehow disengaged from our senses. Just so, there is a technological drive toward virtual reality, to escape this reality through technology. But we are only going further out on the surface into greater deception with virtual reality, not deeper towards truth. Directionally, it will not lead us to wisdom and deeper connection, or to our soul's home. True transcendence occurs through the use of the senses and the body-mind, inward, not outward. In a world that denigrates the body, this truth can appear to be blasphemy.

One word about science (or materialist science which is the form of science practiced in the West). Science does not negate or disprove the spiritual, nor does the spiritual negate science, although it is often presented as an either/or dichotomy. Let me give an example. Sometimes a disease can be worked with on multiple levels. Traditional medicine can be used alongside alternative approaches. Chemical imbalances may manifest in the brain and be addressed by drugs, while the healing can be attended to at the same time from an emotional and spiritual approach. I have personally seen how working on these multiple levels has worked for someone I love. The drugs did not come without side effects, but I believe to this day they served to temporarily stabilize and avert a serious crisis. These kinds of choices are always deeply personal. Fortunately, there is a sea-change happening out there, especially in regard to medicine and the incorporation of the spiritual. Some popular leaders include Dr. Andrew Weil, Dr. Larry Dossey and Dr. Christiane Northrup, to name a few.

My friend Randy Fauver (who wrote the Foreword to this book) has done deep research into how to approach healing to make it more effective, holistic and less likely to cause harm. He has worked with Stanford University, JFK University, California Institute of Integral Studies and The Institute of Noetic Sciences and he lectures widely about his approach. His methodology, called Consciousness Based Medicine (CBM), includes material science as one of the options for healing. CBM turns upside down the conventional model of healthcare, making spiritual and psychological interventions primary and physical interventions secondary. The goal throughout the course of treatment is to assist patients in developing increased connection with their divine nature, with their life purpose and motivation, with other people and their communities, and with the natural world in which they live and from which they gain sustenance.

The CBM treatment protocol uses seven ordered levels of treatment. Arranged in decreasing order of generalizability and safety, and in increasing order of invasiveness and risk, the seven levels are: (1) Spirit, (2) Mind, (3) Body, (4) Touch, (5) Herbs and Supplements, (6) Pharmaceuticals, and (7) Surgery. Each level of healing complements and supports the next, and so would be used in conjunction with each succeeding level of care. Here, you can see, science is not negated—it is included, but only as a part of the whole. I love how CBM puts spirit first, but allows for other options as needed. It is full of choices without the opposition. It honors the whole tree as well as the environment the tree grows in, rather than approaching just a specific part of the tree.

This approach makes practical sense in the game of life, where here are no hard rules. We must navigate through our life daily, sometimes through pretty rough seas, and we have to be aware, listening on a deeper inner level, while smelling the sea, noticing the fish and the birds, and taking in the weather. Our inner compass always holds true to the still-point inside us, and that still-point is what can help us navigate in the outer world. One thing I want to make perfectly clear at the start of this book is that there is no separation of reality. The outside world is no more real than your inner world. Yes, your inner world, your so-called "imagination," is real! It requires no proof. Your experience is real, whether it comes from the outside or occurs on the inside. Yes, you can corroborate outer experience, and that is important when navigating through the political, social, and material world. But your inner experience is just as important, and the balance inner awareness provides has the power to transform our messy world. We have been trained to rely completely on outside experts. There is no one more expert on you than you. Yes, I know the inner world can be tricky and full of deception, just as the outer world is. Deception is built into reality, and accepting this makes it easier to navigate. The antidote to deception is awareness, inside and out.

When things go massively upside down in your life, it is easy to blame yourself. We all suffer and experience pain. But there is a cultural perspective on suffering and pain, and it usually infers that we deserve it, or that it is the fault of others. This creates shame and is not helpful. Suffering has a purpose too. It can help us to learn and grow. It's a pointless use of energy to beat ourselves up about our "mistakes." Sometimes our mistakes are exactly what we need in order to better understand ourselves.

I didn't think I had any intuition at one time. I didn't know how to listen inside. It was only after I studied with the mystic Peter Kingsley that I learned to tune into my inner world. He encouraged me to be present with my sensation and cultivate silence. Only then was I able to hear what my inner self was telling me. The process of moving from a belief (and fear) that I didn't have any intuition, to discovering my amazing inner resource, has given me exactly the experience I needed to compassionately support others in their journey. There was a purpose to my struggle, which I was unable to see in the midst of my suffering. I have learned to be patient.

Exploring the Innerverse

Getting to know how to navigate your innerverse is helpful. Awareness is the tool for observing how information shows up. Intuition (in the form of insights, knowing, and epiphanies) percolates up from the inner roots. It just arrives into consciousness and we can feel the depths from which it comes, and it includes sensations in the gut area. Personally when I close my eyes and tune in, I often see a spinning vortex that psychically exists in and around my gut and goes so deep I cannot see down into it (bringing in the sense of vision here). But I "know" that is where information comes from.

These phenomena can be tremendously difficult to share in words, as there is an ineffable quality to the seeing, hearing, and knowing, but there are a few vocabulary words that shed light on them.

People who pick up on and feel what others around them are feeling are considered *empathic* or *clairsentient*. In my work, I do describe myself as such. To discern my feelings from the feelings of others, I may ask (at an appropriate moment) what they are feeling in order to verify the source. Sometimes those feelings I'm picking up on are hard for me to translate into words because it is such a visceral experience. It has taken untold attention and practice to translate what I feel, and this is an ongoing work in progress.

Through this work, I have become more aware of *clairvoyance*. Clairvoyance is seeing things in inner vision. When I first came across this word, I realized that I had been ignoring many of my inner visions. Part of it was that I had expectations about those visions that were different from my actual experience (born by watching too many movies, reading too many books, and letting others define things for me). As a result, I downplayed their importance or didn't even notice them. The visions were there, but I didn't pay attention to them because of the way they showed up. Giving them more respect has helped my inner vision to become more accessible and expansive.

There have been only a few times in my life that I have "heard" things aside from the constant chatter of my monkey mind. Hearing information is *clairaudience*. It is not one of my primary intuitive modalities.

All of these terms emerge from the same root. *Clair* means clear, as in clear seeing, clear hearing, and clear knowing. The word has different origins. In Old English, it means to fill with light. It is also related to the word *clarion*, meaning to call out. Earlier I described the place from which intuition—inner knowing—arises as the roots of your consciousness tree. These intuitive abilities that begin with *clair* are part of that tree too, but they are more like branches (keep this visual close to heart, as it is central to this book). The next chapter includes some of my own stories and some things for you to think about as you begin to explore what your strongest *"clairability"* is.

Experimentation and experience are your best teachers when navigating the inner world, just as they are in the outer world. You learn by becoming aware of that which has previously escaped your awareness. There isn't anyone who can teach that to you; you simply have to become aware, then trust that your awareness and experience are real and give them the proper respect. They tend to show up stronger when respect is bestowed.

Keep in mind that our attention can be scattered in a world where we are constantly bombarded with information, which can be overwhelming. Our minds grab the information, and we create stories around it based on our past or our fears. This keeps us triggered and distracted, which is the aim of the bombardment. We are easily manipulated in this state, and there are masters of manipulation out there in the phenomenal world.

Persuasion, just like deception, is built into the fabric of reality; and because our minds latch on to patterns to feel safe and in control, our past experience can be the most persuasive factor of all. The past is not a predictor of the future, however. Yes, patterns repeat themselves—they are like habits, and habits can be broken. Sometimes we recreate situations in an attempt to work through traumas that have defined us. However, allowing the past to continuously persuade us can make it a challenge to notice and receive the subtle signals that are happening right now. If challenging, it is also simple. *Remember to be aware.*

The Importance of Patience and Accepting the Flow

You already know that patience has not always been my strong suit from what I have written previously. Because of that, I understand on a deep level why it is so important. Impatience has gotten in my way so many times by now that I can see it in stark relief. Here are a couple of words that stand out as definitions of impatience: *eager desire,* intolerance (of delays, hindrances). Let us examine eager desire. I am struck with an image of a hyper-focused dog, shaking with anticipation for a treat, tail thumping and ears perked. If I place myself in the space of this dog, I lose awareness of almost anything else but the treat I desire. I am single-minded and ready to take what I assume is mine. If it doesn't come my way, I will be highly disappointed, possibly dejected, and may commit a transgression. Unlike with the dog, my human attention will remain on the treat even after it is gone. I will create a story about why it should be mine. The story behind this is that I must have the object of my desire, and if I don't get it, my life, or my day, or my dinner, will be ruined. My over-eager desire is a set-up for disappointment. I am only prepared for one outcome—receiving the treat. Intolerance in this situation is the incapacity to endure anything else except the outcome I desire, which sends me into judgment and about as far away from curiosity as I can get. I am not present, and so cannot respond to the given conditions. I am set up to react with disappointment, thoroughly embroiled in my inner turmoil and judgment, which only sees two possibilities: achieve desire, *good*; desire unfulfilled, *bad*. This leaves no possibility to observe, learn, and adjust.

There is more than one kind of desire. Desire can also be a guidepost when it is connected to the muse that lives deep inside us, but that is not the same as entitled expectant desire, which is more about ego and control. This is the place in which impatience arises and it is a barrier to intuition—like a dam in the flow. Think of it this way: Intuition is a divine gift and it isn't there to get us what we want from an ego level, but rather what we need from a soul level.

Imagine that life is a river and you are an organism in that river. You are meant to go with the flow. The river carries you where it flows. Sometimes there are eddies in the flow, sometimes obstacles. Other times there is so much detritus in the river that the river gets dammed up, but the force of water is so great that eventually the dam will break. The water must flow. You, as just one organism in the flow, do not have much control. What you can control is your attitude toward the river, and your choice to consciously swim with the flow. If you try to swim upstream, you are bound to struggle and eventually wear yourself out. Life is actually a torrent; we are pretty powerless against it, but as part of the water we add to that power and increase our freedom because we are not fighting all the time. There is a truth in the statement "what you resist, persists." If we are fighting the river, we have no energy left for the wonder of following the flow and we make ourselves unhappy.

On the other hand, joy is the natural outcome of consciously going with the flow of the river—and it doesn't mean we don't get bumped and caught in spots along the way. The next chapter is an in-depth exploration of all the known intuitive types—what I call "The Clairs." Through coming to understand your own clairability, you'll sharpen inner tools to navigate the river of life. Lao Tzu once said, "He who knows others is wise, he who knows himself is enlightened." I see understanding your clairability as part of knowing yourself, which enlightens and empowers you to stand strong in any storm, like the majestic tree you are.

CHAPTER TWO

THE CLAIRS

Which Clair Are You?

Clairsentience, clairvoyance and *clairaudience* are the three most common types of psychic or clairabilities, and there are more that are not commonly referred to, including *clairgustance* (psychic smell) and *claircognizance* (clear knowing). I also discovered another, which I call *claircreative*, as evidenced in my experience creating gourd shrines.

Psychic healer and author Echo Bodine helped clarify for me the difference between psychic abilities and intuition. Her clarification matches my experience that intuition is a knowing not necessarily related to one of the senses, but it percolates up from where the senses come together inside our being (as opposed to the surface, which is our physical body). At least, this is how I experience it. Intuition is related to the substance of spirit, which has its roots in eternity, whereas psychic abilities are how information presents itself through our different senses in three-dimensional, time-space reality.

As you dive deep toward the roots of your intuition, it can be helpful to know which of the Clairs is most available to you. As previously mentioned, I am primarily clairsentient, although

I am learning about my clairvoyance and have clairaudient abilities as well. The fourth, according to Echo Bodine, is clairgustance, which is information coming in through scent. I include it here so that you are aware of the possibility, but I personally don't have any experience with it. You can read more about this in Bodine's book *The Gift*.

Claircognizance, the gift of knowing something without reading or being told about it, is not defined by a sensory mechanism. I do not focus on this as a clair ability because my experience tells me this kind of "knowing" is a function of channeling Divine information. Recent research has led me to information about the Alta Major Chakra, known as the Mouth of the Goddess in some tantric traditions. The Alta Major is located at the base of the head, close to the Reticular Activating System, which is your switch for awareness (See Tiffany Barsotti).[4]

The Alta Major is not a well-known chakra; it is not part of the seven-chakra system as it was introduced in the West. It does support my sense of our intuitive capacities and I have written more about it in my blog.[5]

The Difficulties of Interpretation

Before we get into the clairs, I want to bring up a few things that can get in our way. With each clair there is a level of interpretation required. For one, your emotions and desires can get in the way of understanding what your gifts are telling

---

4 Barsotti, Tiffany Jean. 2010. "A Proposed Spiritual Axis of the Body-mind: How the Reticular Activating System (RAS), Vagus Nerve and the Alta Major Chakra May Be the Nexus of Bodymind/Spirit Consciousness." Accessed May 11, 2018. http://www.healandthrive.com/wp-content/up-loads/2017/11/A-Proposed-Spiritual-Axis-of-the-Bodymind-How-the-Reticular-Activating-System-Vagus-Nerve-and-the-Alta-Major-Chakra-Axis-May-Be-the-Nexus-of-Bodymind-Spirit-Consciousness.pdf.
5 Torkildson, Maura McCarley. 2017. "Do You Know Your Alta Major Chakra?" Accessed May 11, 2018. https://www.mauratorkildsoncoaching.com/single-post/2017/03/23/Do-Your-Know-Your-Alta-Major-Chakra.

you. I experience this difficulty when doing card readings for myself. Using these gifts on yourself is harder precisely because it is difficult to be detached from your own emotions and desires. Our bodies are primed for fear as a survival instinct, and fear has great impact on our brain and mentality. I want to emphasize that this is a normal part of human make-up. It is easier to interpret when we have distance from the subject. At times, I can feel when something is off, yet I plow ahead anyway because a part of me doesn't want to know. Either the ego is in control and desires a specific outcome, or I am afraid of the hurt or loss I will experience—in both cases, the outcome is the same: I avoid knowing.

I think there is a cultural expectation that intuitives and psychics should be one-hundred-percent accurate. Yet when are humans ever completely accurate? Just as with science or anything else, there is the matter of interpretation of data. The source may be accurate, but the interpretation may not. We humans get so confused about our own thoughts at times. Why would we assume that we would have perfect clarity in our intuitive interpretations, or that psychics would always be perfect in theirs? It is very important to let go of being right. There is nothing that gets in the way more than this. I came to know this myself, and I also verified it with Randy Fauver, psychic researcher of JFK University and the California Institute of Integral Studies, who teaches his students to let go of the need to be right, and to experiment. Their abilities grow as a result.

Ultimately, we need to make our own choices and take responsibility for them—I don't think it is ever useful to give our power over to anyone. When we give our power away, we cede our responsibility. This is one explanation for the cultural fear of mediums and psychics. We fear their imagined power over us, and yet, often when we go to see a psychic practitioner, we willingly hand over our power with great expectation that they are going to solve our problems for us. We walk away unhappy because we didn't hear what we wanted. Sometimes we turn our unhappiness into discrediting the gift of the medium;

other times we allow unscrupulous people to manipulate and take advantage of us.

I remember going to see a psychic a few years back on a whim. She told me in the session that my biggest barrier was my impatience. I felt angry when I left because she didn't tell me what I wanted to hear. I wanted good news, which was not what I received. Once I got past the anger, which was really a cover emotion for the shame I felt about the undeniable truth in that statement, I was able to use the information to help myself. I *am* impatient. I knew it then and I know it now, and it has been a barrier for me at times. Since that encounter, I have spent years cultivating patience, and still I grapple with it. But in the end, her words were a gift for me. They led me to acknowledge that impatience got in my way, and led me to seek change. Her words only became a gift after I empowered myself to look at the truth she offered and I accepted it on my terms. When I dropped my self-judgment, I was able to work with it. At the very least, now I am aware of when I am impatient, and that gives me a choice to give in to it or not, which ultimately has a positive impact on my decision making. I learned that the choices I make sometimes come with hard lessons, and it is pointless to beat myself up about it. Instead, it is an opportunity to take what we can learn, and see the possibility that our mistakes may have been just what our souls needed in order to learn. Apparently, my soul needs to learn about impatience. On the other hand, I could have chosen to believe that the psychic wasn't really gifted and was just making things up, or I could have taken her words as an indictment and given up instead of taking responsibility for shifting my own patterns.

A Word About Foretelling the Future

I also want to address foretelling the future, because that is often what people seek out in a psychic. Personally, I don't believe that foretelling the future is very useful, and can be harmful. For example, what if someone told you that they knew you were going to die on a certain day, or that someone close to you was going to die or be critically injured within a specific time range? How would that impact you? What decisions would you make? For myself, what comes up is fear. Even if we know what is going to happen, we may not know the how or the why. We will likely try to avoid it, or be terrified, or become obsessed with it. How can we understand the learning that will come from future events? Even if we knew the future, we would still develop a story around it, and possibly become even less present to what is happening. Much of our fear is wrapped around what is going to happen in the future, especially future losses. Our death and the death of those we love is always looming in our future. We lose track of the now when we worry about the future.

My inner guidance tells me that there is nothing but the present moment, always. Everything from our past is always present, as are our ideas about the future. We can only respond effectively to what is happening *now*, in this moment in our lives. We can plan for the future, but we can never really predict it, and our predictions are often nothing more than our fear response hedging against potential losses and grief. It is *in the now* when all our learning and growth happens. The future is nothing but a distraction and speculation. However, most of the popular stories about intuition and psychic abilities present them in the context of knowing the future. We are a culture obsessed with apocalypse, resulting from our Judeo-Christian heritage and linear view of time. Also, worry is a product of our fear system. For that reason, we create dire stories about how we are heading toward apocalypse, then we actually set about creating one for ourselves. We do not even understand the collective power of our mindset. In short, the focus on the future is a distraction.

One last point before getting into the clairs—I feel it is important to share the difference that acceptance and trust have made in my life. My acceptance includes curiosity as opposed to forced expectations. Belief is so often tied to desire. I think of belief as a cheap substitute for experience. Belief can be manufactured and dogmatic, but experience *is*. What the ego likes to do is take our experience and create a belief about it, or make it fit into our current belief system. It is part of our storytelling nature to do this. Being open and curious can lead to new insights and growth. I am free to just observe the experiences that come, and it is quite fascinating.

On this note, here's a tip about getting to know your clairs: What if you allow your experience to guide you rather than making something predetermined out of your experience? What if you approach your experience with a sense of wonder, as if approaching a new world you know nothing about? It is hard to let go of the need to control, and it takes a great deal of courage to let go. Acceptance is a form of surrender, and it takes courage and trust to surrender. The ego does not trust. It is your spirit that must lead the way here.

Now, let us dive into the clairs.

Clairvoyance

This is probably the most well-known clairability. It is the gift of seeing and visions. With clairvoyance, information arrives in pictures. This is the clair that is portrayed most often in our media and the movies because those are visual mediums. Think of the four horsemen of the apocalypse—a dramatic vision of colored horses and riders bringing devastation, famine, and disease. These were potent images of the prophet John of Revelations in the Bible. Of course, this vision has been interpreted in such a way that has led to a systemic belief in apocalypse that has not served our culture, but it is one of the most well-known examples. Dreams are often clairvoyant, but dreams can also be tricky to interpret. Usually, it is much easier for us to interpret the images for someone else than it is to interpret our own. Sometimes it takes sitting with visions for a while, other times the images are quite clear. Often images are metaphors for deeper meaning.

The first clairvoyant image I can remember appeared when I was lying in bed one night, contemplating the way the universe worked. The image of an elephant came to mind. I thought, *Why am I seeing an elephant?* But then I remembered a story I had heard called *The Three Blind Men and the Elephant.* Each man had a different perspective on the elephant that was quite different from the others. This story is a parable about how limited our perspectives are. Suddenly, it made sense that the elephant would come up when I was contemplating how the universe worked. My perspective was naturally limited. As I continued to contemplate the image, I realized there were layers of meaning beyond this initial one. I had a vision of the elephant bridging dimensions. I was barely able to grasp the truth of this even as the awareness passed through my consciousness. These understandings were completely ineffable, and yet the knowing was there underneath my mind's inability to comprehend. I was left with the mystery of it all and in awe. This was a clairvoyant image.

I often get images of things I don't understand. In fact, I am only just becoming aware of how rich my inner landscape of imagery is, and learning how to be aware of it. It is a matter of noticing what I hadn't formerly noticed. One way to describe it is that there are hidden corners in my mind that I am just becoming aware of, and navigating this territory is a whole new experience for me.

When I meditate, I "see" colors and geometric shapes. At times I have seen faces that appear more real than faces in my waking interactions with people. Intuitively, I know these faces are real beings. Perhaps they are communicating with me, and I just haven't been able to understand the message. Sometimes it feels like I'm receiving a quick peek at a divine being, or a "hello, I'm here." I once saw a dragon and was stunned by how real the vision felt. I entered into one of those hidden corners in my being and she turned and looked at me with magical intensity. I didn't feel any danger, but I was shocked. In my shock, my ego protectively intruded and the image fled. I later wrote about this experience in my novel, *The Curious Magic of Buckeye Groves.* I turned it into an experience for one of my characters and expanded upon it. The flow of writing that poured through me was another clairvoyant experience, because the images were vividly there again as I was writing in a state of boundless creativity.

When I put my hands on trees and close my eyes, I am often treated to a close-up view of bark, as if I am moving in toward the tree and becoming smaller, like a bee flying close along the dimensional structure of the bark. After many of these visions, I finally realized that I was seeing with my third eye. I didn't have anyone else telling me that is what it was, and it made the experience more meaningful, the fact that I discovered this on my own.

One time I was treated to seeing golden threads of energy running through the channels in tree bark. This happened after I spent some time sitting with my back against a tree in silent communion. After picking up and walking back the way I came, I placed my hands on the trees in my path as I often do. I stopped at a particular oak tree that struck me as having a lot of personality. With my hands on her trunk, I was graced with this vision of golden threads of light streaming down through the crevices in her bark. I didn't know what it meant in that moment, and I consciously chose not to try to create something, but I pondered it. Once I started walking again, I was suddenly struck with this idea that trees ground cosmic energy from the heavens. This thought wasn't my thought. It came from elsewhere. How I know it came from elsewhere is because it was like discovering an unexpected surprise in my mailbox. I didn't put it there. This is an example of the interplay between clairvoyance and intuition (seeing a vision enhanced by a knowing that percolated up from the depths of my being).

Often things will happen in our outer world to punctuate an inner epiphany. In this case of the oak tree encounter, after the knowing percolated up, I sensed that a nonhuman creature was approaching. Sure enough, as soon as I looked up, first one and then a second coyote came trotting down the hill toward me. Each stopped about twenty feet away and looked at me, then both made their way down into a wooded area below the trail. I was left standing there, fastened in place by awe. It was a seminal moment.

Now, I cannot prove that any of this is not "just my imagination." To be honest, I do not need to. This knowledge has only increased my respect for trees and creatures. I trust my knowing and do not need proof. At a time earlier in my life, I may have passed it off as just imagination, or sought confirmation from a third party. Now I know that imagination is a key part of our intuitive faculties and this time, the experience itself was confirmation enough. Now I am sharing it with you, for you to do whatever you like with the information. It was meaningful to me and that is what matters to me. If my trust causes you to seek more respect for your own experience, then I have accomplished my purpose for sharing it. My hope in sharing is that you will learn to trust your own experiences so that they bring meaning, purpose, and fulfillment into your life. My purpose is not to propose that I know everything about trees from this experience, or how they anchor cosmic energy, or that I have some special knack for knowing when coyotes are going to show up. I don't. I am simply aware at times, and when aware, I am often graced with profound experiences that are personally very meaningful to me and inform my choices about how I choose to interact with the world around me. It enriches my life, pure and simple—no proof required, no need to get it verified by someone else.

To assess your own clairvoyance, start to become aware of the images, colors, and visions that come into your inner vision, and allow them to just *be,* without forcing meaning onto them. This way you avoid the interference of needing to be right. Take time to notice what shows up behind your eyelids when your eyes are closed. This is a good place to start noticing your inner vision. Be curious, but more importantly, accept them as real. Also, pay attention to your dreams. Your dreams are actually proof that you already have inner vision. Practice meditating with presence awareness, and notice what happens in your inner vision as you do it. Paying attention is one sure way to cultivate vision. Take some time to write about games you played as a child. Were there visual elements to your imagination? If it feels safe, try to place yourself in that space again and see what comes up. Take some time to journal about your findings.

If you are not a strongly visual person, do not get frustrated. Clairvoyance is not the only game in town. But I am convinced that we all have access to this gift, even if we are more naturally one type of clair or another. It's a matter of awareness and letting go. Try these suggestions and see what happens as things evolve. Remember, the first step is awareness. It takes time to cultivate your awareness of vision. In the meantime, trust yourself. Any fears you have about not being able to "see" will only get in your way. Also, don't have expectations about how your vision is going to show up. It will cause you to miss how it naturally shows up.

Clairsentience

Clairsentience is the ability to sense feelings. For me, it often shows up as empathy. Another word for clairsentience is being *empathic*. Clairsentience is sensing energy and emotions. Emotions are energy. I get very empathic with my clients. I listen to them in the deep way that I do, with my whole body and being. Oftentimes I feel like crying when I am with clients who are experiencing intense feelings that have been buried because they are painful. I will express to my clients what I am feeling, and ask them if that feeling is true about what they are experiencing. I ask rather than insist. This empowers them to become aware and experience the feeling for themselves if it lands; otherwise it's a good point of clarification when it doesn't land. My experience is that it lands more often than not.

Being able to work with people this way has honed my clairsentience. We need practice to develop our skills. My empathy, when used in service to the client, can be a powerful catalyst for transformation. Nevertheless, I am not one-hundred-percent accurate at all times, and that is okay. I never try to push my sense on to my clients. I simply say, "I am feeling this; does that resonate with you at all?" They become aware and then respond, making the choice to move into it or not. If it doesn't resonate, they push back and say, "No, that is not it, it is this...." It helps them be more aware either way. And I am not obstructed by the need to be right.

When you are empathic and unaware of it, you may feel like you are just plain moody, and your moods often feel unexplainable. This is because you are picking up the feelings of people around you. Clairsentience is often experienced as a sense of something that at first may feel indefinable. I feel something, and struggle with putting the feeling into words. One thing that has helped me is to pay more attention to what I am physically feeling, and to develop my own emotional awareness. I have some exercises later in this book to help you develop your emotional awareness, as that can be extremely helpful, especially if you are clairsentient.

As you are developing this clairability, it can be a powerful exercise to share with others what you are feeling and then see if it resonates with them. Approach it as an experiment, rather than needing to be right and making negative judgments about your ability. Have some patience and you will learn how to hone in your sentience. Keep in mind that the person you are with also may not be aware, or may be in denial about what they are feeling. They might come back to you at a later point and tell you that you brought it to their attention.

Another psychic holistic practitioner, Marta Maria, M.A.,[6] told me that clairsentience is often the most difficult to under-stand, and I agree with her based on my own experiences with it. We are trained to think that our feelings are untrustworthy; that when we have them, they are ours exclusively; and that any unpleasant feelings should be avoided in service to acceptability and objectivity. I never considered that I might be feeling for others too, or that I had special radar for picking up on things. In my mind, I was just confused. Even if I had been aware, I am not sure I would have known what to do with it. Until I worked through my own emotional issues, I was incapable of holding space for anyone else, or even worse, I felt responsible for fixing

6 Marta Martina M.A. 1999-2017. Accessed May, 11, 2018. https://www. martamariama.com.

them or acting out of codependence. Coaching training and certification was a gift because I learned to self-manage, to use my curiosity, and to drop the need to be right, all of which enhanced my intuitive abilities to a large degree.

Do you think you may be clairsentient? I think clairsentience is a lot more common than we imagine. Later in this book, we explore building emotional intelligence through awareness of your body and sensations. For now, begin to become more aware of your feelings and sensations. It is important to start here, so that you understand how your feelings show up physically. Then, notice when these feelings show up and don't make sense in relationship to your circumstances. Ask yourself, is there a reason you could be feeling this way? If not, check in with people around you and see what is happening for them. Does it resonate with what you are feeling?

Here are some other signs. Can you feel a change in the energy of a room when people enter? Are you always hyperaware of people around you? It can be a huge relief when those who are clairsentient realize it, because they stop feeling like they are on an unexplainable emotional roller coaster. I think empaths are susceptible to being overwhelmed, and that can be another clue. Being overwhelmed makes total sense, because an unaware clairsentient has no protection in place and is like a breached levee. There is too much coming in, especially in a world full of people who suppress their emotions.

I was given a practice by Marta Maria that I found enormously helpful for creating a boundary between myself and others. It also helps me avoid taking on and trying to fix things for my clients. The practice is as follows: Repeat three times in a row, "I ask for a pillar of white light to surround me for protection." It helps to visualize the pillar of white light. Notice how that shifts things for you.

Clairaudience

Clairaudience is the gift of inner hearing. This clairability is not my primary, although I can tell you it is my husband's main ability. There have been countless times that he picked up on my thoughts and said something to me that was exactly what I was thinking. I may not give myself enough credit for this ability, as there are always so many voices in my head, many drowned out by my prominent inner critic. Stray, random thoughts come through frequently. It seems to me that discernment can be even more important with this ability.

One clue that you may be clairaudient is that you have thoughts that show up as a form of guidance. I had a clairaudient experience like this when I was in coaching school. My teachers did a visualization exercise with us to help us meet our Inner Captain (inner wise person). In the visualization, the message I received came through as words in my inner dialogue. However, there was a force to them that felt stronger, as if they had come from another place. The teachers suggested that we ask our Inner Captain this question: "What is important for me to know about you?" I got a very clear answer, which was: "I have always been with you." I knew it was true deep in my bones and the response evoked tears of relief. The words were accompanied by a vision of a light being. Some could accuse me of imagining it, or suggest it was just a hypnotic suggestion, but so what? I found it profoundly meaningful and comforting, and it inspired me to trust my inner wisdom. In fact, this exercise was so powerful for me that I regularly use it with my clients.

Maybe this process in the class just made both my clair-voyance and clairaudience accessible through guided med-itation. In the exercise we were guided to a place (our safe place as it came into our vision) to meet our inner wise self, but we weren't told what that would look like or what answers we would receive. Each student had a completely unique and powerfully meaningful experience. What is more important, the meaning or the verifiability of the experience? I'll take meaning. It is my choice. I bring this up to reiterate the im-portance of trusting your experience. There are forces in this world that would rather you didn't. Only you can decide to trust, or not. I want to offer you a different perspective so that you can open up your relationship with yourself in powerful ways. Clairaudience might be one of your skills.

Mental telepathy is a form of clairaudience. My husband saying exactly what I am thinking is an example. This happens a lot when we are driving a distance and are both silently in our own worlds. When I was writing my first novel, I often felt like I was taking dictation for the voices in my head. The book was a combination of my life experiences and inspirations from another place. It was part channeled. Begin to be aware of these instances in your own life. Do you have random thoughts and do not know where they come from? Do you hear voices in your head that you can identify as coming from someone close to you? These all may be signs that you are clairaudient.

Claircreative

I am going to be creative here and coin a new clair. I call this one claircreative. After all, my first intuitive experiences came through my creativity, and I know this is also true for many artists. I would even suggest that this is actually the first and most common clair. There is an entire book written on this subject, although the author didn't name it claircreative.[7] The thesis of the book is that artists pick up and express shifts in our understanding of physics and other sciences before scientists do. This resonates with my belief that the source of our creativity is our divine roots and our subconscious mind, which has access to these roots before our conscious mind. Much information comes in through art. Therapists use art as a methodology to uncover subconscious themes to aid in the healing process, which I believe is all about the soul's journey in this life. Deep healing often transpires in spaces that support the free expression of claircreativity—and the resulting art holds the vibration of the healing for others.

Claircreativity is a clair that is culturally accepted, but not recognized as a psychic ability, except in some circles. Of

7　Shlain, Leonard. 2007. *Art and Physics: Parallel Visions in Space,* Time and Light. New York: William Morrow Paperbacks.

course, throughout history art has been seen as a channel for divine inspiration; however, that was largely discarded with the onset of a scientific worldview, and it is shifting back again, because we can never deny our roots for long. Also, art had to be channeled in a specific way in order to not threaten the prevailing powers that be, like the Catholic Church, for instance. This is why so much art is often subversive.

Here are some questions to ask yourself about your creativity. You may have been claircreative all along and just never recognized it as such. How do you create and how do you view your creative expression? Do you feel compelled to create? Do you have a creative outlet? How do your creative pursuits sustain you, and how do you interact with them? Do they inform your life in powerful ways? And if not, why? How do your creative expressions impact other people around you? Do you feel that art and creativity are magical? Are you surprised by your creations and wonder where they came from? To me, surprise is a clear sign that my creation came from somewhere else. Can you allow yourself to trust that your creativity is a divine resource and see what happens?

Clairgustance

This one will be short because I don't have much experience with it, but I can share some of what I was told by others who have this ability. They told me it can be totally overwhelming. In fact, one friend said she prefers to shut this ability down because it can be so unpleasant for her. She described how being around one of her lovers could be difficult because she always smelled cigarette smoke when with him, even though he didn't smoke. She eventually learned he used to smoke. It made the intimate relationship difficult for her. Another friend told me she could smell death when people around her were seriously ill. Also not pleasant.

Often strong memories are evoked by smell. Is this true for you? Do you often feel overwhelmed by smells, or smell things that others cannot smell? Consider that you may be clairgustant. Begin to explore your sense of smell and be open, allowing your inner guidance to direct how widely you open this channel of clairgustance.

Cultivating Your Clairs

The sharpest tool in the toolbox of exploring your clairability, or clairabilities, is curiosity. One of the problems I experienced back when I didn't think I was intuitive was the fact that my curiosity was suppressed by an overwhelming desire to be intuitive in the way it was presented in popular culture. I also believed that intuition was a gift one either had or did not have. In other words, I thought it was fixed—and therefore my mindset around it was fixed.[8] Because of that, I was afraid to experiment or be curious. I was apprehensive about being wrong. My desire and my belief got in the way of experimenting with my skills, so I was stuck. Add into that potent mix confusion about my own feelings, and the popular cultural emphasis on clairvoyance versus the other clairs, and I had quite a mess to untangle before I could learn to trust myself and my abilities.

As I mentioned before, any skill takes practice to develop. Answer for yourself the questions I have included in each section on the clairabilities. That is a good place to start your exploration. Next, start to notice what is going on inside you. Be open to your experience. Cultivate your awareness as often as possible by surrendering to presence awareness, as I have suggested. Then take on an attitude of play and try not to get caught up in self-judgment, being right or wrong, or having too much expectation. This will allow you to play and observe more freely. You may already have a suspicion about your abilities, and reading this book may have already helped you put your abilities into new, meaningful context for yourself (at least, I hope so). As you experiment, be patient. I remember

8 Read Carol Dweck to explore how a fixed mindset can get in your way. [Dweck, Carol. 2007. *Mindset: The New Psychology of Success.* New York: Ballantine Books.]

my mentor once told me, "Fifty years in the realm of spiritual development is nothing!" You can also go to my website and find my audio "Inner Knower Visualization," and ask this inner wise self for guidance. Above all, the most important step is to begin to trust yourself. Doubt plays a role in our lives, but it usually gets in our way. Self-doubt is often just fear of change, or fear of success and all the vulnerability that comes with success.

Further on in this book, we explore fear to help you understand it and how it gets in the way. We explore when to listen to it and how to work with it. In my case, I was afraid of finding out I didn't have something I really wanted—intuition. I also had really fixed ideas around what intuition meant. We are often terrified of our deepest desires. I make a distinction between the desire of the soul and the desire of the ego. How do I know inside myself when I am faced with a desire of my soul? I know because it simply won't go away. The desire returns over and over and over, and I usually wrestle with it. My ego's desires are more ephemeral. I get bored and move on quickly, and the achievement feels empty and unsatisfying. Our deepest desires come from our soul, and in order to satisfy our soul we do have to face our demons. Don't let that scare you. Your demons are there to test your commitment and to help you learn on a very deep level the truths you would not understand without their lessons. And yes, at times this work of facing demons just sucks! But you are capable. You would not be here if you were not.

The next section of this book covers what gets in the way of using our intuition to its fullest. We will explore emotions, fear, ego, and desire. I place the ego in the section on fear because in my experience the two are deeply intertwined.

BARRIERS TO OUR INNER TREE

CHAPTER THREE

NAVIGATING THE
EMOTIONAL BODY

In this section covering the obstacles to accessing our Inner Tree and working with our intuition, we begin with the emotions and how to navigate them. I want to state up front that emotions are not your enemy! They are a sacred gift. However, like anything else, when we don't understand how to work with them, or relegate them to our unconscious, they can get in the way. Throughout this book, I use the term *emotional body* because emotion is body-based—our bodies help us understand what we are feeling, as well as support our movement through our emotional states. Our bodies and minds are one *Being*, and the body is our instrument of awareness. Unfortunately, we have been taught by our emotionally ignorant culture to disregard our bodies, criticize them, beat them into shape, and wish they were different. This is true both when we are navigating our outer world and our relationships, and when navigating our inner world. Western culture has a curious mix of disregard for emotions and a total fascination with them— think of all the emotional content in popular reality shows, which draw attention to them without offering constructive and life-affirming ways of working with them.

I perceive emotions as part of life's navigation tools. Consider that statement. How does that shift your perception and approach toward emotions? If they are a sacred gift, does that create more room to accept all of them? What if there are no "bad" emotions? I say that with the awareness that emotions can be incredibly uncomfortable, which is why we often want to avoid them in the first place. Emotions are a chemical, physical response to an experience, be it internal or external. Deepak Chopra writes about the author Candace Pert, in the introduction to her book *Molecules of Emotion:* "Her pioneering research has demonstrated how our internal chemicals, the neuropeptides and their receptors, are the actual biological underpinning of our awareness, manifesting themselves as our emotions, our beliefs, and expectations, and profoundly influencing how we respond to and experience our world."[9]

In the West, we have inherited a philosophy that has largely upheld reason or logic over emotion, therefore making emotion a faculty that is "less than" reason. This is part of the package that elevates the mind above the body, rather than seeing it as one of the many senses. In evolution, intelligence has increased with the inclusion of emotion. Mammals have more intelligence than reptiles (although I would argue that so do birds and invertebrates, like octopi). Intelligence cannot exist without emotions, and emotions play a major role in social intelligence. There is no arbitrary separation between reason and emotion, except in the minds of some philosophers. I think we lose the capacity to deal with emotions effectively when we demonize them. We make them unacceptable, thus giving reason to hide them in shame and causing them to perpetuate under the surface. Rather, when we are aware and accept them, they have a tendency to transform into wisdom.

Emotions have a purpose, which is to help us navigate our experiences—to protect ourselves, to process loss, to lift our

9 Pert, Candace B. 1997. *Molecules of Emotion: The Science Behind Mind-Body Medicine.* New York: Scribner.

spirits, to help us navigate future dangers, to experience love and exaltation, and to help us learn. Some emotions need to be uncomfortable or they don't do their job. For example, if fear were comfortable, we might ignore the signals and not respond. Anger, which is an emotion to help us set boundaries, cannot be effective if it doesn't convey displeasure and consequences. Emotions only create barriers when we avoid them. That said, it is good to know how to manage them so that they do not become destructive.

Since emotions are experienced physically, this chapter explores the body as it relates to emotions. Being aware of the physicality of your emotions is one of the keys to emotional management. Managing your emotions will help you with developing your intuitive skills, as well as improve your relationships. Lack of emotional awareness gets in the way of interpreting your intuition, and that is the reason I have included it here. The more I learn to accept and manage my emotions, the better I am able to interpret my intuition and the clearer channel I become. The two go hand in hand for me.

Start with Curiosity

Curiosity is a powerful tool to use with the powerful force of your emotions. When we apply curiosity to our emotions, we can learn much about ourselves in a safe, nonjudgmental manner. Simply said, curiosity about and compassion for what we are feeling lead to healing and growth, especially when combined. This approach is far healthier than judging our emotions, which is largely what we have been taught to do in Western culture. I was told as a child that I wore my feelings on my sleeve, and that I should not show certain emotions. I became ashamed of my emotions. I know I am not the only one who has experienced this. It is a common experience. Is it any wonder that we repress our "shameful" emotions?

Western history is replete with judgments against emotion. Emotion is one reason given for the assumption by some that women are not capable of being leaders. We live in a society that has polarized gender expectations and that has not served us well. Women are dissuaded from expressing anger, and men are criticized for expressing tender vulnerability and tears. This leads to overaggressiveness and violence in men, and a learned helplessness that manifests as victimization of women. This extreme repression is not healthy or sustainable. The truth is, we often make poor decisions when emotionally triggered on account of feeling trapped even though we actually do have a choice. Emotional intelligence is the awareness of emotions— the ability to manage them and make better choices.

Curiosity helps tremendously when we encounter emotions we don't like. We tend to judge our negative emotions, which leads us to ignore them and push them under the surface, where they remain and fester. Rather than judge, try to stay curious about your difficult emotions. I've noticed (both in my own process and in that of my clients) that if a topic is approached with curiosity instead of judgment, it removes the emotional charge of shame and allows more space for exploration. Curiosity creates opportunities for epiphanies that can ultimately lead to transformation and positive change.

Judgment is the tool of the saboteur (the inner critic), the voice that holds us back and keep us "safe." Approaching an emotion with judgment often creates shame and denial, which blocks learning and growth. Curiosity opens up room for self-acceptance, which in turn facilitates learning that ultimately generates forward movement. When we approach a topic with curiosity, we create the space for that process to occur.

The Curiosity Practice

As you experience your emotions, particularly the negative ones, approach them with curiosity rather than judgment, and see what you learn. Keep a journal and write about your experience without censorship. What do your emotions tell you about your possible desires? Be curious about the words you choose; ask yourself what they mean to you. Use your journal to jot down realizations that come from practicing curiosity, both about yourself and about others. This way you can track what you have learned. You may discover that some of the judgments were things you heard as a child. Sometimes emotions can feel destructive, but that does not mean they have to be, especially if we approach them with awareness and curiosity.

I'd like to share an experience of my own, working with a "negative" emotion—jealousy. When I brought curiosity to my feelings of jealousy and envy, it opened new vistas. When I explored what my envy had to tell me about the situation, I found my heart's desire speaking to me underneath the envy, inviting me to answer a call.

This particular experience of jealousy came when I was sitting in an auditorium, listening to a speaker—a woman with an inspiring message and a beautiful presence. As I watched her, I felt the seeds of jealousy arise and wondered, *Why am I not on that stage?* This question was what my jealousy pointed toward as it arose in the thrall of this speaker. The answer was that I hadn't *allowed* myself the desire to be on stage. With that realization, I faced a double whammy of potential judgment—judgment around the desire to be on stage as well as my jealousy of the woman who was up there. There was a back story, of course. I learned as an adolescent that if I wanted to be on stage, to seek attention, it must mean that I was conceited and "full of myself." Even my earlier childhood lessons included the importance of being humble, so to be considered conceited was particularly shameful for me.

All of these beliefs worked against my desire to express myself. However, I am a highly expressive individual. As humans, we all desire attention and opportunities to shine. But there was an implication that if I received attention, I would never ever be satisfied. It meant that there was something intrinsically wrong with me for even wanting it. When we have been starved of attention and approval, we naturally seek it. Attention says we matter, and approval says we belong. It also confers status, and like it or not, we are social animals with all that comes with being social. In other words, wanting attention is normal human behavior. Yet in my childhood world, wanting attention was a bad thing. I wasn't supposed to want it. How did all this judgment of a natural human inclination serve me, or anyone else for that matter? As you can see, it turned it into jealousy toward those who were brave enough to seek attention and receive it. So, in past situations I would have judged myself rather harshly, both for wanting to be on stage and for feeling jealous, and I would have also judged the speaker. However, staying in judgment would have gotten me no closer to either my desire or gratitude for the gift of inspiration this woman offered.

In fact, this wasn't the first time I'd been jealous of women on stage. This was another episode in a long line of jealous moments. What was different this time was that I chose to be curious rather than stay stuck in judgment. Once I uncovered my desire underneath the feelings of jealousy and approached it with curiosity, I realized I was not on that stage because I had not yet risked going there. With curiosity, I looked inside to find and acknowledge the desire: *my expression seeks an outlet, on a stage, somewhere, sometime.* In this moment of jealousy, I could have chosen to tear down the speaker, claim that I could do it better, find fault with all or part of what she said, or criticize how she presented, all while remaining in my fear and judgment about the possibility of getting up on stage myself. The end result of staying in self-judgment is harmful to both parties, because this is often where we go with jealousy— tearing others down instead of looking inside ourselves, and also tearing ourselves down in the process. Instead, this time I chose to look inside the emotion and find the message it held for me: *It is time to express your soul's purpose to a larger group of people.*

Today, I am following that desire—not only am I finding fulfillment for myself, but inspiring others to do the same. Do I still get jealous at times? Absolutely. But I am not afraid to look at it when I notice, and that gives me much more choice around how to respond to the feeling. This is my most poignant personal example of how powerful curiosity can be, and how accepting your emotions as a navigation tool can enhance your life.

Working with the Emotional Body

Now let's dive into ways to increase your ability to manage your emotions. It's particularly important because *emotions arise around our intuitions.* Understanding and working with our emotions increases our ability to have clarity at the same time it reduces denial (which definitely comes up to block our intuition). The blockage occurs not because we are not intuitive, but because we don't want to look at the messages our intuition is giving us. Can you see the difference? Everyone has great capacity for intuition—we just get in the way of knowing what we know for a variety of reasons, and denial is one of them. And when we build our curiosity muscle around our emotions, we also build that muscle to get curious about all of our experiences, even the subtle things we may not have noticed before.

Being present with the physical sensation of emotion helps get us in touch with that emotion in a deep way. When we allow ourselves to experience our emotions fully, we also allow them to pass more quickly than when we "stuff " them, or pretend they are not there, or find ways to distract ourselves. If we don't process them, they stick around, under the surface, often outside our awareness, until triggered. Having been suppressed, the emotions continue to build up over time as we follow this pattern. This explains why, after repeatedly stuffing anger, we can suddenly explode in a way that is out of proportion to the event that finally triggered the release.

I think one reason emotions get such a bad rap is because when we have a negative emotion, we react in a way to relieve the discomfort. These actions are often not well thought out, and we make decisions that we regret later. Learning to accept and ride the emotional discomfort helps. It also helps tremendously to know that emotions pass. I have observed my inner dialogue telling me things like, *I will never feel happy again, or if I start crying I will never stop,* or *everyone will think I am unstable.* We have learned to stuff rather than process our emotions. It is the act of stuffing them which makes them perpetual. The beauty of processing is that we allow them space *to move us*, and then they move on or shift. Having the experience of moving through emotions can build your confidence that they will not destroy you. Knowing they will pass gives us more courage to be with them. Sometimes, moving through an emotion without acting on it can transform our experience into wisdom. We distill wisdom through our experience: emotions are the raw material of the experience, which leads to wisdom.

One time I had a vision about the trap inherent in fighting emotions. In my vision I was in a cage built out of my self-hatred and fear. The more I fought the cage, the stronger the cage became and the more I felt trapped. That cage was a metaphor for the way I was trapped by unexamined and unprocessed self-hatred and fear. I was fighting so hard to avoid the emotions, but wanting to escape them was exactly what was holding me there. When I finally accepted my feelings and let go of the need to avoid, the image of the cage dissolved and I discovered the first glimmers of self-love. This was my first lesson in emotional awareness, and I now know the self-hatred was the result of shame. Sometimes it can take years to fully process a cycle of emotions, or it can take a skilled therapist. Sometimes it also takes more than just psychological work. Trauma can get trapped in the nervous system, and I recommend that if you have severe anxiety and trauma, you find an appropriate practitioner who is well versed in working with the nervous system and trauma. Do not attempt to work with it on your own. We all need the support of a safe container at times.

This brings us to the concept of *processing the emotions.* In order to process your emotions, you need to be able to feel grounded in your body and get to know the physical sensations of the emotion. Each emotion comes with its unique physical markers, and sometimes more than one, because we are physical beings. For example, when I am sad, I feel pressure behind my eyes and heaviness in my heart. It helps if you have practices that involve focus on the body. Here are a few suggestions:

The Body Awareness Practices

1. Take time to get to know your body. Practices like yoga or Qigong (also spelled Chi Gong) are methods many people use.
2. Do the Presence Awareness Meditation practice as often as possible (available on my website).
3. Pause throughout the day and really notice your feet. Where does the floor press into them and where does it not? What is that like? Move your awareness up your body. Notice how gravity feels. Notice the sensations in your fingertips; notice how exquisitely sensitive they are. Touch surfaces. Try to describe the sensations.
4. Take time to dance or move and be aware of how the muscles feel in your body when they move. Notice what feels good and what doesn't. Notice where you feel in balance and where you don't. Push that balance edge a little and hold it as long as possible, and then flow into the next movement (this also helps build resilience in the face of discomfort).

Out of these four practices for becoming more aware of the body, some take more work than others. If you've been in your head a lot, feeling grounded in the body may take more time. Be patient with yourself and keep at it. You may notice some of these practices make you calmer. That's because some of them utilize your parasympathetic nervous system, which is calming.

Once you are able to be in your body, you may find it easier to be with your emotions, especially staying aware of how they show up for you physically. I have been doing this work with my clients for a while now, and I am shown over and over again how capable people are of staying with an emotion, versus repressing it, when they focus on the body. It does require that you remember to be curious and observe; this is why having a guide there to help you can make it easier. I can do this for myself now, without help, because I practice it—and that is a goal of this practice.

Creating Emotional Body Awareness

This next section is designed to help you understand your emotions at the physical/body level, to help you build awareness of your choices on how to respond to them. Awareness will not altogether eliminate getting triggered, but it is the answer to moving through these emotions and being able to work with them. Here are some more suggestions:

1. When you are feeling intense emotions, pay attention to how they show up in your body and stay with it. Eventually, the emotion will pass, and your capacity to stay with discomfort will grow. Use your curiosity. Where do you feel it? What is the sensation? Try finding metaphors to help you understand, as this will often make it easier to identify emotions sooner.
2. Create your Emotional Body Maps (below). The following worksheets will give you an opportunity to map your emotional body. The purpose of this exercise is to help you understand your emotional body so that you can identify your emotional states more quickly, make better choices, and process them more fluidly.

You build emotional intelligence and create choice through awareness of the physical sensation of your emotions. Emotional intelligence expert Daniel Goleman says, "A person excelling in this competence (emotional awareness) is aware of her emotions at any given moment—often recognizing how these emotions feel physically. She can articulate those feelings as well as demonstrate social appropriateness in expressing them."[10]

As I suggested earlier, suppressed emotions have a way of coloring our lives. Emotions are "energy in motion." They are messengers. Tuning into challenging emotions before they erupt, boil over, create chaos, or disrupt relationships is a useful skill and builds our social competence. Being able to experience

10 Goleman, D. 1998. *Working with Emotional Intelligence*. New York: Bantam. p. 55-56.

the positive emotions enhances our health, our relationships, and our lives. Being aware of our emotions and managing them also helps us understand intuitive messages, whether we are clairsentient and picking up emotions from someone else, or avoiding information because it is uncomfortable. When you are aware of your emotions, you can choose whether to express them in the moment; wait, process, and express later; or let them go. Understanding your emotions gives you more choice. It allows you to respond rather than react. Staying with the body during an emotion, especially when it is uncomfortable, also builds resilience, and that resilience creates a greater range of possibility in our lives.

As an example for how this practice works and how it can help us, I'd like to share an experience from my own life. I often experience shame when I do or say something that creates disagreement or discomfort. I hold myself to a standard of being perfect all the time—perfectly attuned and appropriate in my social interactions and never crossing boundaries. Of course, this is an impossible standard that I cannot live up to, but my inner saboteur has this expectation and shames me when I falter. I overstepped my boundaries with a new friend once, asking too many probing questions too soon. My intention was to help, but she read it as intrusive. She responded by letting me know that my probing wasn't appropriate. I was able to apologize and backed off, and we continued our conversation in another direction. However, inside I was embroiled in a paroxysm of self-judgment. When I got home after our meeting, I nearly wrote an ingratiating email to her that would not have served the friendship. It would have been all about my desire to feel better and to "fix" the situation. But something held my hand and I decided to experience the emotion by examining my physical response with curiosity. I experienced an intense band of prickly heat across the region of my solar plexus, and realized that what I was feeling was shame. I was actually surprised by how intense it was. I had never examined my shame, a very common emotion for me, this way before. I stayed with it, allowing myself the experience and stepping out of the story of why I should be ashamed. I was very uncomfortable, but I stuck with it. Eventually, the feeling dissipated.

Typically, after these types of experiences, it might have taken me days or even weeks to "get over it." And yet, in sticking with it, I was able to move on completely in about twelve hours. I eventually wrote an email to my friend. It was both non-defensive and authentic, and she received it with warmth and respect, enhancing our friendship. Now I am able to identify shame more clearly and take steps to move through it more quickly.

Search the Internet and you will find a variety of ideas, research, and systems related to emotions. I believe that we experience emotions on a continuum from love to grief, with fear at the threshold between the two. All the emotions can be traced back to these three. Anger can arise out of either fear or hurt, and hurt is closely related to grief because grief is how we experience loss. Shame is tied to loss (of self-worth), which is turned inward with judgment. For this tree model, I chose the five emotions that I thought would be most useful to building self-awareness. Each core emotion has a branch. The tree sits on top of the mandala which expresses the triad of Grief/Fear/ Love. See the Figure 1, *The Tree of Emotions*, on page 59.

To set the groundwork for exploring the emotions, and to release judgment around them, let's consider a brief description of the purpose of each core emotion, starting with fear.

Fear: Fear is primal and perhaps the earliest emotion to arise in sentient life. It is an emotion of warning. It initiates physical action to prevent loss of life and limb. It wouldn't work if it felt comfortable. Fear is deeply entrenched in our fear system in the limbic brain. When the fear system is set off, it floods our body with stress hormones and temporarily shuts down our thinking brain.

Worry is the planning part of our fear system, and lives in the right prefrontal cortex. Worry helps us plan for potential future dangers so we can avoid danger, and in this way it aids our survival. However, worry is also all speculation. In other

Figure 1
The Tree of Emotions

words, it's about what *might* happen, not what is *actually* happening. One issue is that the modern world and the media are constant drivers of worry. Worry can help us feel somewhat in control, but beyond some planning (like having a safety plan in place), worry is an energy suck. It is our capacity to tell stories that add punch to the worry brain. Our stories can set off our stress hormones, just like real dangers, and we can get stuck in stress. Our body often cannot distinguish between worry and real danger. Overall, fear is all about protection.

Anger: Anger is a boundary setter and often can be forceful to make its point. Like fear, it is about protection (think of a mother bear protecting her cubs). It is also a warning sign that a boundary has been crossed. Whatever happened is NOT okay with us. It helps us communicate boundaries in our relationships. Anger can also be a cover emotion for fear and for hurt. Often, to process emotions effectively, we may need to get to the hurt or fear under the anger, and this is one reason understanding our emotional body is so important. We often feel more than one emotion at a time. Awareness helps us sort through the complexity.

Shame: Shame has the function of inhibiting impulsive behaviors, especially for young children. It helps them learn to adapt to family and tribal mores, to curb behaviors that can lead to trouble, and to gain patience and self-control. For this to occur in a positive manner, a shame response should be followed by acceptance and love—i.e., positive reinforcement. Shame is also protective, and its purpose is to act as a de-escalator when anger and defensiveness could create more danger. Think of wolves. When lower status wolves desire to ingratiate the alpha or de-escalate situations, they take on a cowed shame posture. That posture can instantly flip a tense interaction and turn it into affection. Shame is often the only option for young children in abusive situations. Shame, when it gets stuck, can become one of the most toxic of emotions and one of the hardest to work with. It is important to see the positive aspect of shame to understand the role it plays in our survival, but it is also important to realize how destructive it can be when it has outlived its usefulness.

After its protective function has passed, shame can get stuck. It actually thrives in secrecy. When we feel shame, we are feeling "I am not worthy" or "if they really knew about me, no one would like me." In our shame we want to hide ourselves from the world, and we put on masks, pretending we are OK when we are really cringing inside with severe judgment. The secrecy allows this internal judgment to stay intact. Shame can be completely different for each person.

Grief: Grief is our natural response to loss, and allows us to process changes. I think of grief as the other side of love. It can be difficult to process and the grieving can go on for a long time, depending on the emotional intensity of the relationship that we are grieving. In many ways, we never lose our grief, but we learn to live with it and the intensity can lessen. We grieve all losses, large or small. But grief is also a memory holder. I think our capacity to love is measured by our capacity to accept grief, which is inevitable. Grief is also an experience that can lead to becoming more compassionate.

Joy: Joy is the creative emotion and energy of life. The other emotions are wrapped around protection and loss. Joy is our natural love of living, contributing, connecting, and fulfillment. Joy includes love, happiness, gratitude, and more. I also think joy has an easier, more open channel to serenity, which is why I put it on the main center branch.

Any of the challenging emotions can become toxic if not experienced and processed. Suppressing emotions has the impact of also suppressing our natural joy. They get stuck inside us when we avoid them and they become a filter for all our experience. Building emotional awareness and learning how to properly process our emotions naturally creates more clarity. This is essential for working with intuition.

How to Create Your Body Maps

The purpose of the Body Map exercise is to cultivate your ability to withstand the discomfort of emotions, which in turn leads to having much more choice around your responses and builds emotional resilience. This chapter provides one Body Map form. You can copy it and use it multiple times if you like. Here are the guidelines for using these maps:

- Use your curiosity as emotional states arise throughout your day and become aware of the physical sensations.

- Use your creativity, use metaphors, and use pictures to color, draw, or write that experience on the body form provided. Doing the art helps you to dive deeper into the experience. This isn't meant to be a static picture of your emotions, but rather to help you experience how they show up, and help you stay with it as they move through, shifting the focus away from the story and understanding your body as your guide on a much deeper level. Each time you experience emotions, there may be nuances you hadn't noticed before. In my experience, we often have more than one emotion at the same time, and our sensations can be complex—Body Maps are designed to help you become aware of those complexities.

- These emotional body maps will build your awareness. To help you enhance this exercise I have created visualization audios, accessible through my paid program, "The Inner Tree Courses" at www.mauratorkildsoncoaching.com. The audios provide instructions for use in more detail.

- As your awareness increases, you will find yourself Body Mapping in your mind's eye in real time whenever you have the space to explore. When you are experiencing an emotion, be aware of the sensations and try to stay out of your story about them. If you have time during the experience or later when reflecting on it, create your own Body Map for that emotion.

- Sometimes it's very useful to even draw your own body form, as this can be instructive too (how you choose to draw the form has its own information). Use your creativity to create a Body Map whichever way you want. When I offer this activity in workshops, some people choose to use blank paper, while others use the provided

Body Map or mandala forms. If you have the materials, you can even sculpt your body form.

- As you begin, I suggest creating a *gratitude anchor* (using a Body Map form) to bring gratitude (or love) in to create safety around intense emotions and hold them side by side. This helps knock out any background story that all you are is the particular emotion, or that the emotion will last forever. Gratitude is a safety emotion. It helps us remember that, even in the worst circumstances, we are able to feel gratitude. Creating the anchor makes that a little easier.

- You can use the following instructions for any of the emotions. Just substitute the emotion you wish to explore.

Find a quiet place where you will not be disturbed for at least half an hour. Feel the emotion you are exploring (and if you're creating a gratitude anchor, then think of a person, animal, or place that you feel love for or are grateful for.). We will call this the *focus* for these purposes. Now, quiet your mind by focusing on your feet first. Feel the soles of your feet on the ground. Really notice where there is pressure on the surface of your sole. Feel how gravity pulls you to the earth. Next, feel the sensation in your hands and fingertips. Bring your awareness to your breath. Do not work to change it, just notice the intake and the exhale. Notice the sound of your breath. Notice how it feels as it fills your torso, and how it feels when you exhale. Scan your body for tension, and on your next exhale, release the tension. Do this several times. Next, bring to mind an experience that evoked a particular emotion or your love/gratitude). Allow yourself to really feel what you feel in response. Notice the sensation. Where is it most intense in your body? What is that sensation like? Do you see colors? How would you describe the sensation? Does a metaphor come to mind?

Emotional Body Map

Emotion:_____

Stay with this experience for a moment. Really allow yourself to fully experience it with your body. This will help you retain the sensory information and make it easier to identify going forward. I call this anchoring. After you are satisfied with the anchoring, use a Body Map (or your own form) to draw the feeling. You can also take time to write about it. All of this helps you more easily recognize and respond to your emotions. Awareness leads to choice. When we are triggered, we are not as aware. Be patient with yourself and stay curious. These skills do not build overnight. Use the map as a tool when you recognize you have been triggered, even after you may have already reacted. It will still help you build your awareness and to learn from the experience (as I did with my shame experience).

Now that you have created your emotional Body Map, assess where you are. Remember that it takes time and practice to become more aware. Your emotions will continue to arise in response to happenings in your life. As we know, they can be intensely uncomfortable at times. The methodology I have shared—sticking with the sensation and working to stay out of the story—works amazingly well to ground you in your body while the emotional experience transmutes into wisdom and insight.

CHAPTER FOUR

A DEEPER DIVE INTO GRIEF AND SHAME

We spend so much energy hedging against grief, or avoiding it when it arrives, and yet grief, in this life, cannot be avoided. One of my intuitive epiphanies is that we can no longer collectively afford to avoid grief. We live in a grief-avoidant society, and it is not serving us. Furthermore, I think this grief avoidance has forced the underworld, or our collective unconscious, to hold all our grief for us, and it is now bursting at the seams and may be destroying our ability to create a peaceful world. In light of that, I think it is important to explore grief on a deeper level here.

As I mentioned before, nearly all our emotions can be distilled down to love and grief. Fear, anger, hurt, and shame all coalesce around loss or potential loss—loss of dignity, destruction of boundaries, abandonment, betrayal, abuse—these are all about the loss of something. Fear, anger, and shame are protective. They serve to protect us from loss. Hurt, sadness, and grief occur after the loss has occurred. Fear is on one side of loss, and grief is on the other. Fear of grief is a profound block to our intuition, especially when our intuition is signaling a change (e.g., that it is time to move on from a job or a relationship or any part of our life). Whether change is a choice or is foisted upon us, there will still be grief. If we avoid change because we fear loss, then our intuition cannot serve us. It becomes thwarted. So, it is very important to dive into grief and shift our perspective about it. I will once again use a personal story to illustrate.

Grief is one of the most difficult emotions to process. The deeper the grief, the more intense. In fact, grief may never fully leave us when someone we love dies. The practice of emotional body awareness helped me be with my grief in a way I never imagined, and it became a profoundly transformative experience for me. I used this precise methodology of staying present with my emotional sensations when my father died.

Before he died, my father had multiple myeloma. His imminent death was always on our minds, but he had been doing well and was in remission. Shortly before his death, all of his treatment follow-up tests had shown he was still in remission. He lived in Iowa and I live in California. One morning in August, I received a call before six o'clock a.m. I was asleep, but my husband answered the call and brought the phone to me. I already knew it wasn't going to be good news when he handed me the phone. When I answered, my mother unsteadily explained to me that Dad was in the hospital with an aortic dissection and they did not expect him to last the day. She said he was still conscious and wanted to speak with me. While my stomach hit the floor, she handed the phone over to him. He spoke softly into the phone and said, "Maura, I am so proud of you, of who you are and what you are doing, and I want you to know I love you." I was in shock and at the same time, my heart took in his words. I became aware of how grateful I felt for his love and for the chance to have last words with him. I asked him, "Are you scared?" He quietly responded, "No, I am not afraid to die." I asked him if he was in much pain and he indicated he was. I told him, "Dad, I love you so much and I'm going to miss you. You've given me so much and I know how lucky I am to be your daughter."

There were no further words after that. The room was heavy with feeling. After some moments of silence, he said, "I'm in pain and need to go now." My mother took the phone. She explained to me why Dad had made the decision to refuse treatment and that they didn't know how long it would take for the second layer of his aorta to burst. I told her I was going to get there as soon as I could, and we hung up. I found out later that I was the last person to have a conversation with him. Immediately after our conversation, his outer aorta wall split open, blood flooded his body and brain, and he lost consciousness for the last time.

Before my father's death, I carried stories around in my head about what grief would be like, and about how I would respond to the loss of a loved one. Much to my surprise, my grief for my father did not match the story I had been telling myself about grief. As is typical of the initial stages of grief, I went into shock. I stopped thinking. I was numb and it felt like I was floating somewhere outside my body. I needed help to function. This is also what happens to our brain in the fear response. The prefrontal cortex shuts down. Sudden loss is a devastating blow and our body responds accordingly, as if we are in mortal danger.

Fortunately, I had people to help me. My husband was right there for me and held me as long as I needed. My daughter took charge of finding flights for us all; the same day for me, and several days later for her and my husband. Realizing that I was incapable of making simple decisions, I called my life coach. She helped me plan my packing and figure out any other business I needed to take care of before leaving. I called a few close friends and my clients to let them know I would be away, and I received love and support from all.

I left for Iowa that afternoon, still hoping for more time with my father. They had him on life support, and I wanted to get there before all life left him. I didn't make it. His death was declared at 7:30 a.m. Iowa time, after he had spoken to me, because that was when he lost brain function. They kept his body alive until about 8:00 in the evening. My older brother,

Carl, younger sister, Tonia, and my mother held vigil with him at the hospital all day. After a long day shuttling through a series of airports, I arrived at the hospital at 12:30 the next morning. I wasn't the last; my older sister, Kyanne, arrived from Colorado at 2:30 a.m. after driving long hours. Once she arrived, all four of my father's children and many of his grandchildren were there, gathered around him in a room at Mercy Hospital in Des Moines. We comforted each other, although everyone was in shock. When Kyanne stepped into the room, she looked at him lying on the bed and put her hands to her mouth, saying, "Oh God," and sobbed. "He doesn't look like him, he looks so... shrunken." She tenderly touched his face and kissed him.

After another round of greeting hugs and hushed conversation, we began a spontaneous little ritual, finding ways to say goodbye. My mother called for the hospital cleric to come say last words. I had brought roses from my garden and sprinkled the petals over his body, remembering how he loved our garden when he came to visit. Kyanne pulled his hands out from under the covers, to touch them one last time, saying as she held them, "I couldn't stop thinking about how soft his hands always were." Grateful to her, I made a point of holding his soft hand in mine. My younger sister and my mother did the same. We hugged each other and cried together. As the ritual wound down, we found the resolve to let go and called for the hospital staff to come take his body to prepare it for delivery to the funeral home. We all left together and made our way to my mother's house, every one of us exhausted from the long, sad day.

After the initial shock of his death, it was amazing how my creative self stepped in to find ways to honor my father at his service. Over the next few days, my family came together and shared memories, tears, and laughter. I wrote an obituary and created a memorial website for him. With the help of my parents' pastor and the director of the funeral home, we created a meaningful viewing on Friday evening and a beautiful ceremony at church the following Saturday. These rituals were so important for giving us some closure, and to honor his life and being. My father wished to be cremated and we honored his wish. The funeral home offered many options for urns, and we chose a beautiful urn painted with an image of a path through a forest in shades of green with touches of yellow. The funeral director brought out a catalog for personal urns so we could all (children and grandchildren) take some ashes with us. Flipping through the catalog, I found pages that showcased cremation jewelry. I chose a beautiful silver Tree of Life pendant with a tiny hollow space in the tree trunk for ashes. It seemed so fitting, as my father loved trees too. I have worn it every day since. I stayed in Iowa for a week after my father's death to support my mother and spend time with the family, and to help with thank-you cards and the aftermath. Eventually, it was time to come home. I made a decision to be as conscious as possible with my grieving.

We are amazingly capable beings when we allow ourselves to be present with our grief and each other. This was one of the lessons I learned from my father's death. I let go of the story of being completely devastated by grief. I accepted how strong I was, and marveled at how I was able to cry and to laugh and to function as a whole person. There are many ways in which I feel my father is closer to me. That first year after his death, he was constantly on my mind. I enjoyed that closeness and still do. When I arrived back in California, I decided to stay present with my grief as it surfaced, as it did on the oddest of occasions. I would be going along, apparently just fine, and then it would hit me. Often I felt I was skating on the surface of a great depth of feeling, but I found that pushing to unearth the feelings never worked. I now believe that those periods of skating on the surface were protective. They allowed me to cope with the motions of my everyday life. I had to patiently wait for the moments when the deepest grief would surface. I reached out to find resources, or they were offered to me as a gift from those who understood what I was going through.

A friend pointed me to Stephen Jenkinson's film *Griefwalker*, which transformed my perspective. I wept as I watched it, but it helped me to accept how much I loved my grief as an expression of my love for my father. I understood from watching this film that grief made my love for my father *whole*. The film made that very clear to me.[11] All that we love will someday pass from this world. Grief is an integral part of the circle of love. Somehow, understanding this made it easier to accept. I realized that due to the certainty of grief, it is important to walk through our fear of loss and embrace grief rather than avoid it. It is important to understand this, even while the subjects of our love are still present. I am grateful for the wisdom of Stephen Jenkinson brought to life in the film. Viewing it with the intention to consciously experience my grief also helped me to understand emotion and how to work with it. However, in many ways, those first six months I was only walking on the surface.

Another layer of grief was unleashed the following spring. I was attending a retreat in a business coaching program I was enrolled in, a program my father had paid for a few months before he passed. Before and during the retreat, I was exploring the option of giving up my coaching business. The disappointment I was experiencing over not being able to successfully enroll enough clients to make a living, and my fear of losing my house, had become overwhelming. I had also lost my greatest champion in this endeavor when my father died. At the same time, I was reluctant to let go of the business, because I wanted to honor his gift of paying for the program for me by becoming successful in my business.

I moved through the weekend, full of inner conflict. The pressure for survival was intense. The idea of working for someone else, of finding a job, was tempting. The first day of the retreat I made an announcement to the group that I was looking for work and that I was considering dropping the business. Later, on a break, I signed up to receive coaching from one of the program coaches. I waited for my session outside the coaching room near a group of picture windows. I looked out at the garden and chewed my fingernails. When my turn came up, I sat down and unexpectedly blurted about losing my father and how it was impacting my ability to focus on my business. Soon I was sobbing uncontrollably. In that

---

11 *Griefwalker*. 2008. Directed by Tim Wilson. Canada: Film Board of Canada.

moment, I felt my heart tearing right down through the center, and the periphery of my heart trembled with sensations like electrical shocks—very intense. Fortunately, the coach was a wise woman and she stayed right with me, consciously holding space for me to be in my experience. She provided just what I needed. Slowly, my sobs subsided and I felt a great release. I gave myself permission to not make any decisions about my business right away. Apparently, that permission was just what I needed, because I moved into having more focus and clarity about my business, and decided to move forward with it rather than quitting.

Throughout this process I never wanted to give up my grief. I loved my grief. I still love my grief. I now have more capacity to hold grief. I accept that I will face more grief in my life. This makes me more open and more at peace with life. I do not seek out grief, nor do I avoid it. Stephen Jenkinson proposes that the acceptance of grief is what makes us human, and that until we become human we are still children. He points to cultures with initiation rites that are the entrance into adulthood. These are about leaving childhood and innocence behind and taking the responsibility to embrace the truth that life is ephemeral. We stop blaming, stop making excuses, and stop acting entitled. We become grateful. There is deep wisdom here, and a measure of peace.

How does this shift your perspective on grief?

It's not a perfect process, but when we decide to stay present with our emotions, particularly grief, we find we are strong enough to withstand them. We have an inner core of strength, which is a divine gift. I don't believe that Love would ask us to bear more than we are capable of. It is we who decide we are not capable. It is we who decide that emotions are unbearable, unmanageable, and not to be tolerated, and in doing so, we create our own incapacity. We avoid allowing emotions to perform their purpose: to help us navigate our life, learn, and be in the experience of life. I believe that avoidance and judgment also lead to shame. Of all the emotions, shame is the one that can become the most toxic.

The Problem with Shame

While I don't want to demonize shame, just as I don't want to demonize any other emotion, I do have strong words for it. Shame is probably the most difficult emotion to deal with, because by its very nature it wants to hide and keep secrets. Shame has its proactive purpose. At a primal level, shame is protective in that it de-escalates volatile situations. Think of wolves subjugating themselves to the alpha wolves. The posture of shame is head down, seeking invisibility. It does the job pretty well, actually, although it is not the only de-escalation strategy around. Shame can save our lives when we are incapable of defending ourselves, when we are physically weak, when we are small children, or when we are at a disadvantage physically. In the animal world, it prevents a fight to the death (animals often posture, and one will move into shame posture to de-escalate to avoid injury or death). There are times when resistance could lead to our demise or much greater bodily harm, and in these cases shame is a survival strategy. But shame can quickly outlive its usefulness. It is important to remember that shame can be a life-saving strategy so that we don't judge ourselves for the times we may have gone into shame. Understanding that it is a survival strategy can help us heal from perpetuating the toxic shame that results from trauma and abuse.

On another level, shame can also occur when we are trying to be someone other than who we are, as if what we are is not good enough; or it can arise when we compare ourselves to others and expect perfection from ourselves. It becomes destructive when we hide it. Like our other emotions, shame needs to be processed in order for it to pass. The problem is, shame prefers to hide in the corner while we resist the vulnerability required to share it. Outside the gaze of our conscious awareness, it festers like a low-grade infection, sapping our life force. We assume that others will judge us as harshly as our inner judge. To add to the mix, we confuse vulnerability with weakness. In fact, it takes great courage to be vulnerable (see Brené Brown).[12] Paradoxically, once we allow ourselves to be vulnerable, suddenly we are no longer vulnerable because what we were hiding is already disclosed; our dreaded secret is already exposed and we no longer need to hide it, and can face the circumstances. Before disclosing our secret, our fear-bound mind creates all sorts of stories about what will happen should our secret shame become known (all these stories are only speculation unless they actually occur). Once exposed, there is no choice but to accept, and we can face reality rather than spend energy avoiding. There is a kind of relief that occurs here; room to breathe again, room to breathe through. Often our story is much worse than the actual reality we face when shame is finally exposed, as we are usually much harder on ourselves than others are. We may find that we get compassion from others rather than judgment.

Shame is also the shadow side of trying to be perfect. Holding ourselves up to a rigid model of perfection, and expecting that we will be able to achieve that perfection, is a set-up for disillusionment. Because we can't be perfect, shame will coalesce around our "imperfections." The more we try to be perfect, the more distant we will become from our authenticity, the more we create barriers between ourselves and other people, and the less we are open to going with the flow. The need for perfection is destructive to our inner worth and our ability to trust ourselves. It is important to talk about shame in the context of intuition because it is very important to recognize and deal with shame to help clear pathways to intuition. Be careful of creating expectations of "perfection" around your intuitive skills also, as that is one of the biggest obstacles to keeping those pathways open.

My intuition bloomed during coach training because the program creators consciously fostered experimentation and set a ground rule of "no right or wrong" in the context of our learning. They encouraged us to blurt out our hunches, and to let go of them without judgment if they did not land with

---

12 Brown, Brené. 2015. *Daring Greatly: How the Courage to be Vulnerable Transforms the Way We Live, Love, Parent and Lead.* New York: Avery, Reprint Edition.

our clients and each other. The instructors' role modeled this in class and throughout certification. I continue in this vein with my clients. If my intuitive blurts hit home, then that can be very useful for my clients. If they don't land, it still creates a jumping point for the client, helping them to better clarify what they are feeling or experiencing, even if by contrast. It's a win/win as long as I don't force my interpretations on the client or get defensive about it. If I get attached to being right, I will no longer be in service to the client. If hunches don't land, that doesn't negate my intuitive ability. No one is one-hundred-percent accurate at anything all the time. In addition, whatever came up may be just what the client needed to hear. As long as I stay focused on being of service, setting my ego agenda aside, then the process can flow. There is great freedom in not needing to be right or feeling shame when wrong. That is trust at a deep level.

In regard to disclosing shame, it does make a difference with whom we choose to disclose our shame. And it also depends on the subject of your shame. It is generally not a good idea to disclose to someone you know will be triggered by your subject. Choose someone who can hold a more compassionate view. It is important to pick someone who is capable of listening with empathy. There are some people out there who thrive on shaming others (a likely sign that they have much shame themselves), or they are unable to "be with" for whatever reason—usually that has more to do with them than it does with you. So choose a confidant carefully, either someone you know loves you and whom you can trust or, if needed, a professional.

Most of the time I have found that the things I am most ashamed about are a non-issue for others. They don't judge me quite as harshly as I judge myself. Let me give you one example of shame in my life, and how I dealt with it. I've chosen this example because in this instance, I was conscious of the shame and chose to explore it with curiosity.

Remember the shame story I disclosed earlier in this book? We can use that to explore a little deeper. When I met my friend, I was practicing my coaching skills in almost every conversation. I found it hard not to practice. Fortunately, she was very good at setting boundaries, and when she told me she felt I was being intrusive, I apologized and we switched the conversation. She moved on. I did not, although I covered it well for the rest of the evening. The truth was, I felt deeply ashamed about my mistake, holding myself to a standard of perfection. When I left the dinner I walked back to the train with a sinking gut, feeling nauseated and beating myself up for being so "stupid" (here's a great glimpse at a trigger word my inner critic likes to use). By staying with the sensation, I was able to identify that I was experiencing shame. When I eventually decided to email my new friend, I made the choice to make myself vulnerable and tell her how ashamed I had been, and I apologized for being intrusive. This was different, more real, than my first apology during our meeting. She accepted my apology, writing that she appreciated my honesty and integrity, and that she could see I was a thoughtful person. She also said that she had completely let it go after my first apology and that it had been a non-issue for her. What I realized is that sometimes shame skews our perception about the gravity of things. It makes them appear much larger than they are.

I don't think we can completely avoid shame. We exist in such a shame-based culture, and it is part of our emotional make-up, but we can cultivate emotional awareness and compassion to release it, heal, and move on. It doesn't have to control our lives, as it once controlled mine. Shame once played such a large role in my life that, in my younger years, I severely restricted my voice to avoid being wrong and feeling stupid and ashamed. I take a lot more risks now, and that includes trusting my intuition rather than listening to my inner judge. Working through my shame allows me to love and accept myself as I am, flaws and all. In working with clients, I realize that what I love most about other people is their beautiful imperfection—all the places they are human, vulnerable, and so courageous.

Loving and Accepting *You*

Loving yourself is the key to resilience. Accepting that you are worthy of love and that you are part of God, Source, the Universe (or however you name that power in your life) is most empowering. Your life has its own pattern and flow. You are one strand in a symphony that is completely unique and a necessary part of the whole. Your life has a purpose. Deep inside you, you know what that purpose is. Your purpose doesn't have to be complex. Sometimes we overcomplicate things, and then we get in our own way.

Loving myself has allowed me freedom. I have the freedom to be who I am, to be completely authentic, warts and all. When I love myself, I am not afraid of being unworthy anymore, and that gives me room to experiment, to fail, and to learn. This is what it takes to learn how to use your intuition and to trust it. You can't understand how it works in you if you aren't willing to take some risks. When we are so focused on being right, that comes from a lack of self-worth: "I will not be worthy if I am wrong." When you love yourself, being "wrong" is just part of the journey of learning. In fact, when we make mistakes, or things don't go well, we learn deeper.

I've been facilitating training of one kind or another for over sixteen years now, and what I have observed is when students struggle with the material, they learn more. They learn how and why, and they also learn why not. Errors can lead to great insight. Mistakes can lead to learning, which is most important for us. However, if we are so busy judging ourselves about our lack of perfection, we lose the opportunity to learn from these errors and mistakes. Part of self-acceptance is honoring the courage it takes to try something different and to take risks. In a culture that expects perfection, making mistakes can be very risky. Making a mistake is *failure*, and failure is a shame-laden word that conjures up rejection and banishment. Since one of our most compelling human needs is belonging, the threat of not belonging is terrifying; and when failure is judged harshly by society, we are set up to find ourselves unworthy when we fail.

In many jobs, you only get so many mistakes before you get fired. Sometimes one mistake is enough. For many people, getting fired from a job threatens their survival. One of the reasons public speaking is one of the top fears is because the prospect of making a "mistake" and saying something wrong, or looking stupid, is terrifying to that part of us that wants and needs to belong. Our body experiences fear the same, whether it is imagined or real. Loving and accepting oneself includes also loving the parts of yourself that experience fear, that need to grieve, that need to belong, that need attention, or need to be admired. Those are all normal human needs. Loving yourself means loving it all, including your shadows.

Loving ourselves creates room for joy. Self-acceptance means *I unashamedly love what I consider to be the best parts of me too.* When I think of joy, I realize that it is the small things that sustain me, the little joys. We are culturally set up to look for big, dramatic successes and we often miss how important the small joys are.

For example, when I was traveling for one of my corporate jobs, I went to the diner in the hotel where I was staying to eat dinner. Each table in the restaurant was festooned with a single gerbera daisy in a small vase. The flower at my table was red. Dinner alone was always a great time for practicing Presence Awareness and in that dreamy space of being immersed in presence, I glanced at the gerbera daisy in the center of the table. I visually dove into the flower, noticing the variety of petal shapes that created an intricate, complex pattern of texture, light, and shadow in living color. I gazed at this wonder with complete awe. Moments like these remind me of when I "discovered" water as a child, which occurred one day when washing my hands. Entranced with the flow of water, I surely wasted gallons of water, enjoying its cool, liquid caress over my hands, its ability to flow effortlessly around them, and the way it disappeared down the drain on its way to everywhere. Moments like these bring pure unabashed joy and their lasting impact in my life is testament to their power.

Recently I took a class, *Awakening to Our Fairy Kin,* offered by my friend and priestess Marguerite Rigolioso. During the class she led us through a visualization to meet our fairy ally. In this visualization, after traveling through the veil to the magical forest of the Fae, I met my fairy ally. My ally appeared in my inner vision like a Brian Froud pixie (if you want a visual, look up Ffaff the Footer). He/she (the gender is very fluid) revels in silliness. We were led to ask for the ally's name. Mine said, "My name is Ally Sheedy." My initial somewhat abashed response, *"What? That is the name of an 1980s actress."* On further reflection I realized the ingenuity of the name. The name Ally, a direct reference to ally/supporter. Sheedy references the Irish name for fairy folk, *The Sidhe* (pronounced shee). Ally (alley) is also a passage way, or portal from one place to another, as in *he is my portal to fairy land.* The multiple meanings of this name confirmed for me Ally Sheedy's validity and I giggled with glee, thrilled to have my new inner friend.

Ally Sheedy has been with me ever since. His entrance into my life is much like the return of a lost childhood companion. Ally's silliness is my joy. He likes to sit on the hot tub cover when I am soaking. He sits on the edge of the hot tub cover, torso-less, showing only his swinging crossed legs adorned with his favorite Pippi Longstocking-type leggings and pointed fairy shoes. Other times he dances a jig for me. Occasionally she shows up in pink fairy dresses (gender shifts intentional here). I am compelled to honor him every day at my fairy altar under our oak tree in the backyard.

I share with my family what Ally Sheedy pops in to say now and then. My daughter Megan thinks I am nuts (secretly, I think she relishes my strangeness). My mischievous side adores the expressions I get in response. This puckish silliness is an inheritance from my father's side of the family. Growing up, Megan was often subjected to my inane whims when I drove her to high school in the morning. I regaled her with different voices, accents, and crazy characters, much like my father used to do when he was driving. Like he did, I relished the responses—rolled eyes, shaking head, "my crazy mom" cringes. I once asked my partner, Pete, why he never teases me about my relationship with Ally Sheedy, the latest addition to my repertoire of eccentricity. He sighed and responded, "I like having you around, so I just accept it. The alternative is sending you off to an asylum and that is not acceptable."

Ally Sheedy is real to me. I know this is unconventional in this world, but I love my relationship with Ally Sheedy and all the unfettered joy it brings me. My self-love allows me to accept and express my peculiarities even if they make me vulnerable to the criticism of naysayers or people who think I should act like an "adult." Joy is the natural result of childlike wonder to the small things we often miss when adulting. In fact, I need this joy to sustain me in the face of the state of this world. Like all other emotions, joy (and its offshoot silliness) is our birthright as humans and I refuse to deny myself my unique forms of joy for the sake of convention.

Our emotions—every single one of them—are part and parcel of the experience of being human. It comes with the package and our souls understand their importance to our growth even when our minds do not.

CHAPTER FIVE

WORKING SHADOWS

What is a shadow? Shadows are the parts of ourselves we find unacceptable. These parts can be negative, but they can also be positive. Here is a Jungian definition of shadow from Wikipedia:

> *(1) an unconscious aspect of the personality which the conscious ego does not identify in itself. Because one tends to reject or remain ignorant of the least desirable aspects of one's personality, the shadow is largely negative, or (2) the entirety of the unconscious, i.e., everything of which a person is not fully conscious. In short, the shadow is the "dark side."*

Even though the shadow gets a bad rap as the "dark side," there are positive aspects which may also remain hidden in one's shadow (especially in people with low self-esteem). Contrary to a Freudian definition of shadow, therefore, the Jungian shadow can include everything outside the light of consciousness, and may be positive or negative.

Shadows as Teachers

What is the value of shadow work? When we confront our shadows, they lose the power they have over our lives. Shadows and shame often go together. Because of shame, we tend to avoid looking at our shadows. Yet shadows are part of our soul's contract for growth and clearing in this life. Remember that your consciousness is a tree. The shadow is the part of that tree that you lack awareness of.

Living trees sometimes have burls and indeed I've seen many grandiose redwood trees with them. Burls are growths on a tree that often are the result of injury, viruses, or fungi. Burls have a deformed grain. They can grow on the trunk or the branch and can be filled with knots and dormant buds. Your shadows are like burls. They have grown inward, are dense, and are hard to see. We grow shells around them to protect ourselves from seeing them, and then we project them onto other people. Projection is classic scapegoating, blaming, or accusing others of what we don't want to see in ourselves. Sadly, this doesn't rid us of our shadows; it just makes them more destructive.

But did you know that burls from trees are coveted for their grain? They are prized for their beauty and are used for veneers, inlays, and special handcrafted objects. Once your shadows are brought to light, they can also become prized. If you think of your life as a masterpiece, the shadows lend contrast, depth, and beauty to that masterpiece.

Shadows are our unwanted children that need our love. The story about jealousy that I shared earlier is a story of the shadow. My jealousy was a reflection of my desire to share my story and wisdom. Part of the shadow was my very human need for recognition, attention, and regard. By denying those human needs, I created a hungry ghost that was going to drive me to seek it out, perhaps in unhealthy, unconscious ways, which is what we often see happen with performers who seek fame as a means to find self-worth and end up becoming self-destructive because the fame can never fill a lack of self-love. Inside my desire for a stage was the gem of authenticity that I had to share with the world, a gem that no one else could offer except me. That desire goes deep. It comes up from the depth of my roots. But it is not mine alone. We are all connected to the Divine Creator, and the gifts we bring into this life come from Her, and are rooted in Her. Who are we to think that we should not embrace them and share them?

This is one of the purposes of community, to share our gifts in service to the whole. If we deny this, we are also denying it to the community. Often our shadow is the seat of our power and leaves us terrified of acknowledging and owning that power. To acknowledge it means we must become responsible to it and can no longer hide. It means that we have to grow up and quit depending on others or God to save us and protect us. We want to stay a sapling in the sheltered sunlight, but our soul wants us to grow tall, all the way to the very top of the canopy, so that we can bask in the full sunlight of our being.

In the myth I shared at the beginning of this book, *Inanna and the Huluppu Tree,* Lilith is one of the shadows that must be removed from the tree in order for Inanna to stay safe in her sheltered garden. Inanna allows the tree to be cut down and hands over her power to her brother and lover. Lilith is the shadow of Inanna. She is the wild, untamed power inside Inanna that has become unacceptable to the domesticated world. She is untamed sexuality. She is autonomous. She is self-aware. As Marianne Williamson points out in her work, we are far more fearful of our power than we are of our inadequacy: "Our deepest fear is not that we are inadequate. Our deepest fear is that we are powerful beyond measure. It is our Light, not our Darkness, that most frightens us."[13] If you remember, Inanna bemoans the fact that the tree is holding these shadow characters. She sees them as a problem. They are getting in her way, and she wants to rid herself of them, not realizing that they are part of her—the powerful, self-determining part of her. By allowing the Huluppu tree to be cut down, she literally cuts down her connection to her roots and hands off her power.

---

13 Williamson, Marianne. 1992. *A Return To Love: Reflections on the Principles of* A Course In Miracles. New York: HarperCollins.

What Inanna didn't understand, and what we can learn from this story, is that our instinct is always untamed, as it must be. Our instinct flows with that which is present, while our minds want to hijack that flow and force it to conform to the ordered garden. The mind is not capable of capturing the flow for long, and when it does, it distorts it. We also distort our shadows so that they appear to be evil. We distort our power, learn to fear it. Women's power is not just the power to give birth and nurture, it is also the power to shake down that which impedes life from its sacred task to change and grow.

Working with Shadows

Curiosity is the best tool for working with shadows. It will be extremely difficult to work with your shadow without dropping your inner judgment. It is your judgment and the judgment of others that has kept your shadow hidden in dark corners. The original sin is the sin of judgment against self and how we are made. Shadows can be different for everyone, but of course we have cultural shadows as well. For example, one of the biggest shadows we have culturally is sexuality. Sexuality has been subject to repression and control for thousands of years, with the most adverse effects on women. Women carry the burden of sexuality as sin, and are held accountable for both their own sexuality and that of men. Somehow it is okay for men to be out of control sexually (in fact, this is expected) and women are held accountable for inciting and exciting men. Women are called names and blamed for rape. If we risk being more sexually uninhibited, we are called sluts and whores. For the most part, the more promiscuous men are, the more status they gain. Not so for women. This has led to a particularly destructive form of pornography that victimizes and abuses women. This is a great example of how destructive shadows can be when they are unexamined. It's like our denial of the shadow is a force that twists the natural expression of the human sexual experience into something as negative and potentially toxic as most pornography is. In believing our sexuality is sinful, we have made it just that—toxic.

Working with shadows means examining both the cultural shadows, which we all inherit, and our personal shadows, which come from our personal family history and experience (peers can have great influence here too). In my case, my family history and my peers informed a belief that wanting attention was a bad thing. The message doesn't always have to be explicit. A statement such as "you just want attention" said with a certain inflection and posture can imply enough to create a maelstrom of shame. I don't remember exactly how this message was conveyed in my family; what I do know is that I took it deep into my body. Later, this message was highly reinforced in my adolescent years. There was a word for it in my peer groups in middle school: conceited.

This word, *conceited,* was tossed about freely and sometimes on a daily basis in the gossip among the girls at my school. Whenever a girl showed any confidence, this word was used to condemn that confidence and put the girl back in her "place." That place was insecurity, not visible, demure. Some of us were more susceptible to shame around this than others. I was one of those. That word used against me was like a gunshot in the gut. It took me down and wounded me on a deep level. My response was to retreat and hide. Other girls in my class had more confidence. If criticized, they didn't stay down long. Or sometimes they played the game differently. They could take down others with fierce gossip and seemingly remain unscathed—or so it appeared to me at the time. Little did I know that bullying is a sure sign of insecurity and a lack of self-worth. I will say that they knew how to play better than I did. My defense was to retreat and lick my wounds. I carried these wounds into adulthood. They showed up again as jealousy. My jealousy was the toxic expression of my desire for attention and acknowledgment of my worthiness.

The truth is, I love to be in the limelight, and it also terrifies me. My fear is that I am too much. A desire, once repressed, creates a hungry monster that, when unacknowledged, becomes the gaping maw of "never enough," a hunger perpetually unsatisfied. This monster can take over your life in the form of judgment of others, manipulation, condemnation, and self-hatred. I hated myself for wanting attention. My shadow material always threatened to make my friendships a potentially abusive playground. I almost lost a good friend as a result. Fortunately, she was both compassionate and truthful with me.

Here is another story in this lineage. One night I had a dream about her. In the dream, she was working to make me famous. She was connected to resources that I needed in order to become famous. Her importance in my dream was all about getting me what I wanted—fame. I told her about the dream one day when I was over at her place, and I think it must have been the last puzzle piece for her. After I shared the dream, she told me she felt unseen and used in our relationship, and that she didn't feel safe with me anymore. She announced that she wanted some space from our relationship. After hearing her words, I was devastated. I cared about her deeply, and the last thing I wanted to do was hurt her and make her feel unsafe. But my shadow had come between our relationship, and I was, on a conscious level, completely unaware of it. Now, made completely aware by her honesty, I left her place and went home. I sat on my couch, stunned and in shock. As the shock wore off, I started to weep and I wept until the tears dried up. It was as if the weeping cleansed me and created new space inside my being to look more honestly at what had happened.

Sitting on my couch, exhausted and drained, yet also still and spacious, I heard a voice. It said, "I hate you. You are so stupid!" I winced, surprised. To be hearing this voice inside my head so clearly was a completely new experience for me. It was so clear it was almost audible outside my head. At the same time, I knew it had been there all along, but now I could actually hear it. I was shocked to experience the reality of it. This voice was toxic, unrelenting. But now, consciously aware, I thought, Wow, this is what I have been saying to myself? How does this help me? By this point in my life, I had been exposed to the idea that loving myself was important to my well-being. At that moment, seconds after I heard this voice, loving myself became possible. A compassionate, wiser part of me stepped in to say, "This is not good and it does not serve you." This compassionate part saw beneath the shame I was experiencing and allowed me to see the shame for what it was—the expectation that I was going to be a perfect friend or never make mistakes or cross boundaries in my relationships.

It took me a much longer time to make amends toward the part of me that wants attention. That one is still a work in progress. I have bolstered my awareness by educating myself about what it means to be human, and how the importance of belonging plays such a strong role. So does self-expression. Back then, I didn't have the training I have now around cultivating curiosity, which was something I picked up in my coaching certification program. The coaching program helped me build that muscle. Now I can consciously apply curiosity toward myself, as well as toward others. This doesn't mean I do it perfectly and at all times. Being completely human, I fall into judgment, most particularly around my triggers and wounds. But the curiosity helps me be aware of them and move through them more efficiently. The truth is, some things may always trigger me. A desire for fairness is built deep into my bone structure. It was also a trigger for my father. It is an inheritance, so is unlikely to go away. When things feel unfair, that is when I step into judgment. Knowing that life will never be fair doesn't change my make-up. But awareness gives me both the ability to pause when I get triggered and choose my response.

Upon applying curiosity to my desire for being on stage, I was able to peel off even more layers of judgment to come into a cleaner relationship with that desire, and to begin to see that perhaps the desire might be more than vanity. It might just be a calling. By calling attention to myself, I call attention to an aspect of being human and I normalize it. By owning that desire, I call attention to it for others, and model the opportunity for them to own it for themselves. I know from my own life experience that I am not the only one who has judged myself harshly for wanting attention. Because the need for attention is a common shadow, the monster that results creates the narcissists that carry it, creating all the more reason for many of us to disown this part of ourselves out of fear of becoming that narcissist.

Looking back at my adolescent experience is also a testament to how women can turn this shadow against each other. This thread of jealousy is a common thread among women, and it is one that divides us. It comes up over and over again. We have been trained to condemn each other for our beauty, for our sexuality, for our need for attention, for being perfect, for being mothers, for not being mothers, and the list goes on and on. We can never be good enough, or we have to worry about being too good and becoming the brunt of the jealousy of others. It is an impossible tangle.

Patriarchy uses this dynamic to its advantage. It is the perfect weapon against our solidarity. And so far, patriarchy has largely succeeded in one guise or another. Patriarchy dismantles the possibility of women's solidarity by eliminating our ability to trust ourselves or each other. It also disqualifies our inner experience as false, so we cannot even turn to our own inner wisdom for support. Patriarchy also actively destroys emotional awareness, always questioning the value of emotions that fall outside the acceptable range for each gender.

Even jealousy, actively cultivated between women in a patriarchal system, cannot be self-acknowledged. To admit it would be leaving ourselves too vulnerable to judgment and even expulsion from our tribes. Jealousy tears apart our friendships, tears up our relationships and families, tears down our celebrities and icons, and makes our workplaces a bed of landmines. It is the shadow side of desire. When our desires become shadows, they often show up as jealousy. When we can acknowledge our desires and shine the light of our consciousness on them, they lose their destructive shadow power and become a beacon to guide us into awareness of our nature, deepening our wisdom.

There are all kinds of shadows for all kinds of humans. My desire for attention may have been a big shadow for me, but that may not resonate for you. What are your shadows? Can you throw the light of curiosity on them?

Shadow work is some of the most important work we can do, for our health, for our cultural health, and for the survival of our world. Working with the shadow also opens our ability to see more clearly, both in our outer life and our intuitive inner life. Robert A. Johnson has written, "When we consciously approach the shadow, we examine a very powerful aspect of our personality that is almost universally shunned and avoided. In this way, we enter the realm of paradox." He elaborates on paradox: "To transfer our energy from opposition to paradox is a very large leap in evolution. To engage in opposition is to be ground to bits by the insolubility of life's problems and events. Most people spend their life energy supporting this warfare within themselves. To own one's shadow is to prepare ground for sacred experience."[14]

I will add, to work with and own one's shadow also cultivates resilience.

The Role of Suffering and Finding Resilience

Let's face it, to live life includes suffering. Look around you at the world, at nature, and you will find suffering. Suffering has a purpose and plays a role in creation. It is we who turn the story of suffering into a negative, and that is a justifiable response because it can be incredibly hard to deal with suffering. Our bodies naturally resist suffering, and our bodies inform our minds. Furthermore, suffering and trauma often create a dynamic in our body that makes it difficult to thrive, cultivate a positive outlook, and live a fulfilling life. There has been a lot of recent study on the impact of trauma on the lifelong health of those who have ACE (Adverse Childhood Experiences) scores.[15] It is not as simple as "thinking positive" to overcome these impacts. Healing can require deep work with

---

14 Johnson, Robert A. 1991. *Owning Your Own Shadow: Understanding the Dark Side of the Psyche,* New York: HarperCollins.
15 Nakazawa, Donna J. 2015. *Childhood Disrupted: How Your Biography Becomes Your Biology and How You Can Heal.* New York: Atria Books, Reprint Edition.

both the body (nervous system) and the emotional and mental self. Our beliefs about our own personal suffering are also impacted by cultural beliefs. Here in the USA, suffering is seen as punishment and is used to punish. We have made suffering a shadow. When we make suffering a shadow, it takes over our life. Suffering becomes a reason to shame. We create a story that those who suffer deserve it for some reason, whether it be karma or laziness. However, we don't grow without challenge. What if suffering (challenge) is not something we experience because we deserve it? What if it is part of the structure of the universe? What if challenge, dissolution, and loss are all part of creation and the creative process? How does that statement impact your response to the suffering in your life?

When we believe we deserve to suffer, or that we made a bad choice or did something "wrong," we naturally go into defensive mode and carry shame around it. We resist our suffering, constantly hedging against it. Our resistance only serves to harden our suffering. Acceptance softens it. Our souls grow through the process. Bliss can be experienced even in the midst of our suffering if we let go of our resistance.

I realized that for much of my life I had been living in a state of waiting for the day when things will be better—the day when my ship will come in. Once I worked through challenges and reached acceptance in one area, I saw how this belief showed up somewhere else in my life. It prevented me from being present, from acceptance, and from taking all that I could from my experience *now*.

I am not personally a Christian, but Christianity and Jesus play a large role in our society, and how we understand his story has a huge impact on how we view being human. What if Jesus came not to save us from our sins, but to show us that we can still trust God/Life through our suffering? Did he not suffer? Did he not doubt, and did he not ultimately trust in the end? One version of the story (Jesus came to save us from our sins) comes from a space of our childlike need to be taken care of, and the myth of "happily ever after." I've noticed how hardened and judgmental this particular version can make of many of its adherents. In that version, suffering is a huge shadow looming over everything, and those who do not follow the "perfect" word of God deserve to suffer. You don't have to look far to see that playing out in our politics. The other version (to teach us to trust in spite of our suffering) asks us to grow up and become responsible for our own souls, and to be compassionate toward self and others in the process. This version helps to shed that judgmental mantle and encourages humility. This is actually what I believe Jesus taught with his life. It is our compassion, especially compassion toward self, that creates resilience. Acceptance, coupled with compassion, strengthens our ability to persevere. If we want to create a better, more compassionate world, we have to stop waiting for God or Jesus to save us. We have to take responsibility for our own salvation.

I think so often intuition is approached as if it is the key to preventing our suffering. But this approach is one sided and leads to obscuring our vision rather than enhancing it. It does account for why we sometimes will not see what we don't want to see. If our view of suffering is one of complete opposition and avoidance, or of shame, then we will not even look at the potential in suffering. When we avoid embracing the whole of life, our roots can no longer nourish our trunk.

Suffering will happen. Suffering is always about loss of one kind or another. What we resist persists, and if we constantly hedge against loss, we have already created our own suffering. If we tell ourselves the story that we cannot bear suffering and loss, and we believe that story, we create more hardship for ourselves. It is amazing what we can withstand when we have faith in something deeper, when we know that the story is larger than us. It gives new meaning to our suffering and makes it somehow more bearable.

So, how do we bear our suffering? One way, which I wrote about earlier, is to be present with the emotions as they arise, being with the body while the expression of the emotion passes through us. There is great wisdom in this approach, as it allows the energy of that emotion to move. It helps tremendously not to judge ourselves harshly for our suffering. Freedom comes from being nonjudgmental. Recognizing that we carry in our bodies stories about the meaning of suffering is important. This perspective on suffering informs our ability to deal with it; the other causes us to resist and perpetuate it.

Finding support as we release the shackles of the shadow is also very important. There is no question about the role empathy can play when you are suffering. Suddenly, you are no longer alone. Support helps us feel connected. Connection and belonging are some of the deepest human needs. Empathy helps us feel like we belong and that we are understood, that we are important. All of this can help relieve some of the suffering, or make it somehow more bearable. Author Stephen Jenkinson says the biggest fear about death is the fear of being forgotten, that our lives did not matter. Our lives matter when they impact other people, when we belong and contribute and share love.

I've been in close contact with my mother since my father's death. She has been experiencing some health issues and pain. I know it is much harder for her to bear her pain without my father there to empathize with her and take care of her. Her aloneness impacts her ability to manage. All of my siblings and I pitch in to support her and provide an ear for her whenever she needs it. We have come closer together as a family around the loss of our father. None of us is alone with our loss. We listen to each other, we share our feelings and experiences of missing my father and also feeling him near at times. That provides comfort, meaning, shared experience, and context for our own private grief.

Over the past few years, I have had many moments when I felt despondent and hopeless surrounding his death. I learned to ride through these moments, realizing that those feelings would pass, new things would happen, and life would move on. In those moments, I often wanted to give up, throw in the towel, and stop trying, but I didn't let the despondency of the moment drive my actions. Often I would call a friend or a coach/mentor to help me through those times. I also cultivated a practice of gratitude.

Studying how our "protective" fear system works helped me to understand that the mind naturally gravitates toward the negative as a defense mechanism. By looking for things to feel grateful for, I tracked the positive while my nervous system did its thing with the negative. It helped bring balance and hope. I looked with curiosity at the stories I was telling myself, and asked questions of them. Were those stories part of a habitual pattern of negative perception? Were they really true? Or were they a projection into the future and speculation? The answer was that they were more often a projection. If there was real disappointment or loss, I could choose a different story about why one thing or another didn't work out. (Note that in the case of failure, it is important to balance out and to learn from our errors, and to be honest about our part in them without making ourselves wrong or bad.)

Suffering is an integral part of our emotional life, and I hope I have given you an alternative perspective to help balance out your accumulated concepts about it. Confronting shadows is also a major path to growth. The only other thing I want to add is that it is very difficult to do this work on our own. The support of others is critical when doing shadow work. It is both important and a courageous act to ask for help. Even in your darkest, meanest hour, there is enough love in this universe to fill you completely, and fill everyone else too. Love is the endless well of creation, even in destruction.

Next we will look at fear and ego, as these can also be major barriers to intuitive knowing. But before we delve into this, let's take a moment to understand the importance of integration, the mind-body-centric process of recovering the felt sense of being whole.

Integration

When we dive deep into the body and mind, and all the emotional content there, we can begin the process of integration and movement toward wholeness. In a patriarchal culture, the female body is not a safe place to be, and in shadow work we often stumble upon mental structures in our unconscious that were established to protect and keep us safe. Most of these structures were created during our youth, when we were unable to articulate and integrate our experiences. Below is a piece I wrote after a process of integration that was particularly empowering for me. It demonstrates how I unearthed certain shadows in the process and integrated them.

> Over time we learn that the female body is not a safe place. When our body is not a safe place to be, life is an existential crisis. We need to be in our bodies to fully participate in life. If our bodies are not safe havens, we can never fully participate because our energy goes into protection all the time. So often that protection is also turned inward. As women, we learn to constantly monitor and remain on high alert for the things that make us vulnerable; or we dissociate and leave our bodies, stop listening to what they have to tell us, and then no longer *know*. We stop ourselves from knowing. This is my story of not knowing.
>
> Working with a healer friend, I gained access to a huge monolith in my core. It reminded me of the monolith in *2001: A Space Odyssey*. Inside was all my knowing and underneath that, all my hurt. Both were locked together—all the things I didn't want to know because it hurt. Even seeing this monolith brought me to terror. Opening it up took a great deal of courage, but I did. All the presence awareness meditation I have done over the years helped. So did allowing myself to choose when and how. I brought safety to my fear by becoming present.
>
> At first I warily circled the monolith. My gut attempted to ward me off, but I decided I was going in. Opening the monolith was at first devastating, yet it was no more than I could bear. Part of the devastation coalesced around the "idea" that I had to act, to make an immediate decision about what I should do in

response—but once I faced it I realized I didn't have to DO anything. I could stay with the feeling, experience it, and bring safety to it. My safety. Presence. The monolith had tightly bound all the feelings I ignored, allowing me to pretend I didn't have them, helping me hide from myself.

Opening the monolith was step one. The next step was meeting the menagerie. You see, I have all these different parts of me, namely characters that have their own roles to play in my protection. Many of them rely on old rules. They still play the game the old way, a way that is not serving me anymore. The cast of characters includes, for starters, the School Marm. She is harsh, rules with a stick, demands I conform. She tells me it is necessary for my survival. She also needs proof, so suspicious she is of anything new. The problem is this: I am the one that pays for her methodology, for dancing with her is the scared Little Girl. She doesn't trust anything new either; she listens to the School Marm and her experience of protection is all with Marm. She likes to hide behind School Marm's skirts. Then there is Dragon, but she gets ignored. She is the one who sees and knows. She has the power of momentum and she can fly. She knows too much that could be dangerous to any masks of denial. Little Girl doesn't trust her (but is coming around). Next there is Warrior Priestess. Her methodology is to fight and she does it well. Unfortunately, she often turns that fight inward. Then there is the Shapeshifter. Shapeshifter has the magic to navigate, shift, and morph into the stance for protection. In childhood, she used shame, silence, shapeshifting and hiding, even from herself. She is incredibly tired, as she is on all the time. Her tactics worked, once upon a time. I survived. Shapeshifter works unconsciously and has no fun. She needs fun. I also have Lion, the fierce predator that can go after what I need, but Warrior Priestess has been stabbing

her in the ear, trying to protect the Little Dog. I haven't
figured out Little Dog yet. Little Dog is also part of my
menagerie. I have more to learn.

My healer told me I needed an A-Team and all
parts of me must be in agreement about who is on the
A-Team. The A-Team is my team for safety. Finding my
A-Team meant meeting my menagerie, which opened
up many a can of worms as I learned about each facet
of this motley tribe. Which brings me back to the core
feminine wound. It was during this shadow work when
I realized that existence is terrifying, and that insight
brought me straight into my body and sexuality. At
first, more terror mounted. My body is not safe. My
body is the receptacle for shame, for ridicule, for
molestation, for potential and actual rapes, for being
sinful...and the list goes on and on. My body isn't safe.
But all *Knowing* comes through the body. How can I
Know if my body isn't safe? No wonder Dragon gets
ignored and Shapeshifter works so hard!

You see, as a woman in a patriarchy, I am wrong
in my body all the time. Let me list the ways in which
women are held to be wrong. We are wrong when we
are sexual, when we want pleasure. We are wrong when
we don't wish to give pleasure and when we are blamed
for being raped. We are wrong when we dress this way
or that way. We are wrong when we fight back or stand
our ground; then we are considered most dangerous
and are called witches or bitches, at times burned at the
stake and accused of killing babies. We are wrong for
having a body that gives birth. It makes us too weak to
be decision makers, and it is our "burden" for sinning
because our seductive bodies are supposedly the root
of all evil. We are wrong when we feel and wrong when
we don't. The feelings we are allowed are restricted to
those that are safe for others. We are wrong when our
feelings make others uncomfortable. We are wrong
when we don't nurture and we are wrong if we nurture

too much. Every way we turn we are wrong. Our bodies are wrong, making us targets—justifiable targets in the system of patriarchy; justifiable scapegoats who must always carry the burden, for everyone, of being in bodies and yet always unsafe in them. When our bodies are not safe, we can have no self-trust and we can't know. To *know* is to be in touch with your body and your feelings, and trust is a feeling of safety. So often as women, our knowing is cloistered behind monoliths and our protection is turned inward. We are colonized, even inside ourselves. *Malignant shame,* my healer friend calls it.

What patriarchy does to men is a whole other topic, but it makes them fragile—too fragile for women to be allowed to be whole. The problem is if we are whole, too many men perceive they have much to lose and do everything to stop that, both consciously and unconsciously. We, however, already lost everything at birth. Being female, we learn to pretend, to wear masks and to shapeshift in order to navigate the daily gauntlet we must face in these female bodies.

This is existential crisis. We feel life isn't safe and we have to be vigilant, turning protection on ourselves, cultivating harsh School Marms to keep us in line and Shapeshifters to help us navigate the landmines. We must hide our hurt from everyone, including ourselves. We may have a Warrior Priestess who occasionally comes in to protect us, but even she may turn on us, especially if our inner fierceness threatens to hurt others when we listen to OUR feelings.

Facing this menagerie, I howled and then wept, sobs shuddering the length of my torso. The monolith had been broken open. And then the trail of crumbs led me to revisit the many memories of when I was hurt and shamed for having a body, for being female.

It's not as if I hadn't visited these things before in therapy, with good friends, and with body work. But this time, for once, I felt my female hurt all the way to the core—the wound raw, open, moving, and shifting. Hours later, I focus on safety, negotiating my A-Team and climbing out of the abyss. I am learning on a deeper level how to take care of me. My Little Girl is placing her trust in Dragon.

This is a powerful example of my shadow work. As mentioned before, shadow work is challenging, sometimes terrifying. It is important to have help, whether that is therapist or a friend who can hold space with compassion while you are facing the darkness. Once again, the best I could do here was to share my personal experience.

Everyone has different shadows. There are common cultural links, but the specifics of how they show up may be different. The power here is in the integration. When we brave looking at our shadows and accept our humanity, we find great freedom. Shame and shadow go hand in hand; when we let go the shame around our shadows, we can relax. We can heal. One of our biggest cultural shadows is the ego, and fear. The next chapter dives into how those two things are related.

CHAPTER SIX

MANAGING
FEAR AND EGO

Fear and craving—these are the two biggest impediments to intuition. You may think you are just not an intuitive person or that you lack the capacity for intuition. As I have suggested, you first need to learn how to listen within. But even once we learn how our particular intuitive powers work, fears and cravings can still get in the way. I prefer to use the word *craving* here rather than desire, because I like to think of *desire* as coming from our divine roots, and therefore view it as being holy. But craving can be a whole other can of worms. It is more akin to addiction. When we crave, we want something outside ourselves to fill a hole, which of course it never can. That hole can only be filled from the inside. But that doesn't stop us from trying to fill it from the outside with money, accomplishments, drugs, a perfect body...and the list can keep going. Both fear and craving prevent us from seeing and accepting what our intuition may be telling us. Often it is an unhealthy and unmanaged ego that drives craving and fear, getting in the way of flow. As I stated earlier, we need an ego in order to take action in this three-dimensional, material world, but we must always be aware of what it is up to.

This chapter will help you gain some perspective on ego and its relationship with fear. I draw from my many years of education for this chapter, but it is not based on formal theories of ego. There is no shortage of information and theories about ego, from Freud to Jung to Rappaport. I draw from my own experience and awareness, which comes from years of studying the ego, from my own behavior to my alternative education as well as my work with clients. I use the word *ego*, but perhaps it is more accurate to define my use of ego as pertaining more to self-image or identity.

Looking at the Ego

The ego is an insecure creature to be sure. It is ephemeral. It is a part of you that is not eternal, like your body is not eternal. One way to think about the ego is that it is a construct, an identity. The identity is constructed from a combination of past experiences, reflections from peers, mentors, or parents. The ego is also full of needs that involve status and identity. It is the psychology of having a body with its desires and needs, and it is also the construct of being a social animal, so society has a huge role in the development and maintenance of the ego. I believe the primary purpose of the ego is protective. The ego is all about survival, survival of the body and the sense of self. Its primary goal is to protect the social self so that we can survive, thrive, and grow. The ego is our social fear system and is linked to our physical fight-or-flight system through our storytelling brain. It works in conjunction with the body and is part of the body. Our body includes a nervous system, and that nervous system is embedded throughout our physical body. In the majority of cases, the ego dies with our body when its time comes. It is aware of this and it desires to be in control and immortal. It *must* want to live, otherwise we would not protect ourselves as we so carefully do, and surely would perish much sooner. Alas, the ego is not meant to be immortal. We live in a world where physical death is embedded in nature. In third-dimensional reality, death is the great recycler. In transcendence, like a snake shedding its skin, we eventually grow out of this skin. However this makes the ego, which cannot exist without a body and its creature comforts, insecure.

I think the ego gets a bad rap, and honestly, it can do some bad things, so it has earned its reputation. But consider this: its job is to protect us. One of the deepest human needs is belonging to the tribe we are part of. Not belonging is life threatening, so the ego plays an important role in our survival. It also includes the drive to thrive and it looks for opportunities to do so. Like other social animals, humans have a social pecking order. Those on top of that pecking order have a better chance at thriving. The difference with the human social pecking order is that we create a story around what it should look like and what it means. That story can look very different from tribe to tribe. Here in Western society, we confer status on wealth and having lots of things. Yet the potlatch cultures of the Pacific Northwest conferred status on those who gave away the most. In addition, in modern culture we can have multiple levels of social order and value. For example, at work, status may be about appearances, showing up with a "get-down-to-business" attitude, whereas in our hiking club, status is about how many trails we have hiked.

We have many more choices in the modern world than we did in the world we evolved from. At one time, our one tribe was *it* and the threat of not belonging *in it* was life endangering. Our nervous system has not changed much since then, and neither has our need for belonging, even though there are more choices for where to belong. When our belonging is under threat, our fear system kicks in and we feel threatened and insecure. The most dangerous force in the world is insecurity. Animals are at their most dangerous when they feel threatened, and so are we. When our social self feels threatened, we might respond with rage, especially if we have not developed emotional maturity or experienced unconditional love at some point in our lives. The ego moves in to protect us and may choose to harm others to maintain its position. But that does not mean that the ego is always a bad thing or always makes bad choices. Still, the human collective tends to remember the negative and so the stories of egos out of control and causing great harm are remembered for a long time. Think Hitler, Pol Pot, etc. However, in matters of day-to-day life, we survive because of our ego and for that we should be grateful and happy to have it.

It's no secret that the ego also likes to be comfortable. That way it can coast along, feeling secure in its position, even if that position is not very secure. It knows that position and feels safe when all is in order. The unknown is threatening to the ego. That means that sometimes being a victim is a comfortable position. Egos can develop status around victimhood too. I've both seen it and done it. Think about people competing around who has suffered the most, and you will get my meaning.

The Remedy for Dealing with the Ego

Contrary to what the ego would have you believe, there is actually a remedy for the ego. Just as it is important for parents to provide two-year-olds with guidance to be safe and to grow, the wiser part of ourselves must also take responsibility for the childlike ego. Awareness, as with everything else in this book, is the key. Staying aware of what the ego is up to gives us choices we don't have when it is running on autopilot. The ego is also a creature of wants. This is also a must. In a healthy ego, pleasure—be it through touch, food, play or rest—is how we thrive and stay vital. In order to feel good and secure, the ego seeks pleasure and avoids pain. Because belonging is one of the deepest human needs and is necessary for our survival, positive attention and nurturing are important for our ego's sense of security. It is most important that we are loved and well cared for as children, and given boundaries in order to have a healthy ground for the ego to develop into a self-managed social participant.

Having no limits can be just as destructive as excessive limits. Without pleasure, the ego can grow an unhealthy need for negative attention. Such is our need for attention. Even negative attention can seem better than none at all. All of our experience and history goes into our ego. It protects itself however it can. It is important to remember that. It is also important to know that some strategies of the ego come from childhood experiences that were not healthy or nurturing. Those strategies were protective at the time, but those same strategies often stop working long before the ego is ready to let go of them. Part of our growth may require getting help to nurture our egos back to health.

As I started my journey to heal from egoic patterns, the first therapist I worked with explained to me that the healing path was an upward spiral. We may have to return to something over and over to completely heal it, though each time we return, we return to a higher place on the spiral, different from the last time. We are different and so is our healing. I have found this to be true for over thirty years now.

There is another way to look at this from the work of Roberto Assagioli, an Italian psychiatrist and pioneer of transpersonal psychology.[16] In his work, the "I" is the being that experiences all the modes of consciousness. Empathic love, the kind of love that accepts the full range of personality aspects, allows the "I" (which includes consciousness and will) to feel fully seen, therefore synthesizing the whole of thoughts, feelings, sensations, and subpersonalities, leading to what I would call wholeness. The "I" remains disidentified (another word for identified is attached) from specific contents of the personality. In contrast, an identified "I" arises from an environment that does not accept the whole, but only a limited range of the personality. This creates a survival personality, causing dissociation from other aspects of the personality. The unhealthy ego is the identified "I." A healthy ego does not need to limit its identity and can flow, as well as pick and choose how it desires to show up. Much of our ego problems arise because

---

16 Firman, John and Gila, Ann. 2007. "Assagioli's Seven Core Concepts for Psychosynthesis Training." Accessed May 11. 2018. https://www.synthesis center.org/PDF/Seven Concepts.pdf.

the "I" is attached to a specific range and the rest of the self is hidden from awareness. This can lead to many issues, including identity crisis and rigidity.

Once the ego receives unconditional love, we can mature on a deeper level and begin to transcend the identified ego, allowing our wiser self to become the driver in our lives. Because most of us have wounded children within us that never received unconditional love, we carry those small children inside of us with all their needs.. However, our wiser self can play a large role in caring for the wounded child and can lead it to healthy integration. It is a dance. It is part of being human that sometimes we do this dance well, and other times we let the ego get too identified and rigid. It is usually from this dance that our greatest soul lessons are learned.

The Relationship of Ego and Intuition

This gives you a little background as to why the ego can get in the way of listening to our intuition, especially when our intuition is telling us something contrary to the ego's desire to remain safe and comfortable in its limited identity. It does not handle change well because it is a threat. Our egos construct stories about how things should be and set up expectations to match them. Along with those stories about how things should be are stories about how things should not be. The world doesn't usually cooperate with the identified ego in its quest to remain tucked safely in its comfort zone. Thus we experience challenges to "play bigger" throughout our lifetime.

Societies also have a collective identified "self," and each culture has its own stories about how the world should operate and what we are capable of as beings. One of those stories, which I wrote about earlier, has to do with the purpose of suffering. Suffering is often looked upon as a form of punishment. As children, we are rewarded when we are "good" and punished when we are "bad." We are also taught that to want some things is good and to want others is bad. Structure is necessary for the smooth operation of society; however, it can set up an internal conflict, as wanting is often a physical impulse. At any rate, in our society we learn to see suffering as a punishment and pleasure as reward. We become good children to be rewarded and we are trained to avoid pain.

I don't think we should seek out pain, but the avoidance of pain, which is discomfort on one level or another, seeps over into our psychological make-up. Our bodies feel pain, whether it is physical or emotional, so we naturally avoid emotional discomfort as well as physical. Whenever we avoid something, a story about our ability to bear discomfort arises and that story often looks like this: "I cannot bear pain." This is aggravated by our cultural avoidance of emotions. We have been at war with our emotions for thousands of years. The problem is that when we can't accept our emotions, we bury them. The ego gets identified with not having certain emotions and buries them. When we bury them, they tend to stick around and build up under the surface until the pressure becomes too great and they explode, seemingly out of our control and possibly creating a path of destruction in their wake. This only serves to validate the war on emotions, and so it continues in a self-perpetuating cycle of suppression and explosion (or depression), reconfirming the belief that emotions are more trouble than they are worth. Of course, I am speaking in generalities and not everyone is like this, but it is a cultural belief that is thankfully beginning to change.

Because we have categories of good desires and bad desires, some of our desires often become shadows and we don't allow ourselves to be aware of those that fit the category of "bad." Bad desires do not fit into our identity construct, but of course they exist and there is still a drive to satisfy them. That drive has to be twisted and justified by the ego so it will fit the identity, and this is where deception plays a role. This is how we can mask so much from ourselves.

When we crave what we want, we believe our happiness is contingent upon receiving what we want. We can build up an arsenal of stories and expectations about how having what we crave will serve us. We may think that achieving our goals will satisfy our craving. The truth is that the identified ego is never satisfied, and can never be satisfied. Achievement is ephemeral. Those stories can range from "I won't ever be happy until..." to "I deserve to have this..."and "If I don't get this, I won't ever be happy, satisfied or successful." Sometimes the opposite can be happening underneath: "I want this but I don't really deserve it," or "It's not possible for me to ever..."

If we can love and demonstrate compassion for the identified ego and thus help it dissolve into our wholeness, we are much more open to the signals from our intuition, which is part of the whole of our experience and, I believe, connected to the Self that is the Divine Universe. We are able to become less rigid and go with the flow. This is why it is important to look at ego and its relationship to using your intuition to a much higher degree. Let's bring Assagioli back in here for a moment, because his description of the "I" allows us to see ego as consciousness and will. It is the observer who experiences (consciousness) and who can direct observation (will). This is what my presence awareness practice opened up for me—the ability to be a much less identified ego and gain access to becoming whole, to knowing that experiencer, or the awareness, on a much deeper level. I become "the one that experiences."[17] I believe that one is my soul.

The Fear System

Our bodies are set up with a well-designed fear system to accomplish our protection. We have a lot of mythology around fear culturally. Fear, especially for men, is seen as a liability. Men work hard to never show vulnerability. Our heroes are seemingly fearless, always stepping in danger's way to protect others (think Superman, Captain America, and so on). However, complete fearlessness means something is wrong with the brain. It's neither healthy nor desirable. A true hero's courage is a choice in response to fear. Courage asks us to face our fear.

17 Firman, John and Gila, Ann, *Assagioli's Seven Core Concepts for Psychosynthesis Training.* https://www.synthesiscenter.org. p. 11

It does not come from a fearless place; it comes from a determination not to compromise what is important to us. It is the natural outcome of taking a stand for what one values.

Here is an overview of our physical fear system. I think it is important to have an understanding of how it works to help us set aside judgment around our fears, so we aren't faced with a double whammy: having the fear, and then judging it. And looking at the number of posts on Facebook about the importance of being fearless, I bet many people are internalizing the judgment often implied about being fearful, especially when it comes around our need to belong. Most of the posts I see about fear seem to be critical of this need to belong, which commonly shows up as worrying about what others think about us.

Please note that I use the word *fear* to cover both fear and anxiety. Our fear response is rooted in the middle of our brain in two almond-shaped groups of nuclei called the amygdala, which is our emotional center and is connected to the hypothalamus. The amygdala is on constant alert for signs of danger. All of our senses have direct input into the amygdala. If it receives any signals it interprets as danger, it immediately sets off the fear response by activating the hypothalamus. The hypothalamus activates the autonomic nervous system, which has two components, the sympathetic and parasympathetic. The sympathetic nervous system activates the adrenal glands to provide the body with a burst of energy for fight or flight, including pumping hormones such as epinephrine and cortisol into the bloodstream. Pulse rate and blood pressure go up, breathing becomes more rapid, the lungs open up, and our senses become sharper so that we become more alert. All of this revs up the body to respond quickly to danger. In addition, the prefrontal cortex is temporarily shut down—meaning that the thinking brain is taken out of commission. If we think too much, we might overthink the danger and fail to get out of the way or fight back in time. The amygdala also holds memory, and it holds on tight to memories of danger in order to keep us out of danger. What this means is that our negative experiences can be very sticky. The brain sticks to the negative as a survival technique.

The whole fear system is very complex. After the danger has passed, it is the parasympathetic nervous system that puts on the brakes to dampen the fear response and bring us back to resting awareness and engagement. The energy of fear or anxiety can get stuck in our nervous system, and this is called *trauma*. Trauma typically arises when our fear system is activated, but the situation has immobilized us. For example, we were held down for some reason and are unable to respond with fight or flight. Small children are powerless to fight back; adults may also enter situations where it would be life threatening to fight back—in both cases, the fear system includes a freeze response. Even though the victim freezes, the body is still activated with all the adrenaline, increased heart rate, and rapid breathing. That energy needs to be released. Animals naturally shake this energy out once danger has passed. Humans can inhibit the process. The energy of fear can get stuck as trauma, and trauma has a way of taking over the brain and body. Trauma creates hypervigilance, and the amygdala can get activated by sensory input that reminds the person of the original trauma, creating flashbacks. The body holds memory as well as the mind. Memory of trauma can be preverbal and inchoate, making it hard to process and easier to activate. Trauma can cause victims to be unable or less able to function socially and connect with others.

A shut-down prefrontal cortex is why you can't think as well under high levels of stress. One of the most common fears is of public speaking. The reason why people go blank on stage is because the fear response comes online and reduces the ability to think. This fear is a social fear; speaking out publicly can threaten our belonging. This is also one reason why it can be so difficult to be vulnerable, to be authentically ourselves, especially when it goes against the grain or we believe it goes against our tribal beliefs, which feels like it literally threatens our belonging. In many instances, this can still be life threatening. This is why rejection is one of the most painful experiences.

I see a lot of my clients beat themselves up over needing to belong and looking for status within their social groups. I have done this myself. We somehow imagine that we shouldn't care what others think. The idea that we can be completely independent is not realistic. Exile and isolation lead to emotional and physical trauma, and eventually death. If only we understood how important it is to belong, then perhaps we wouldn't beat ourselves up for feeling devastated when our belonging feels threatened. I hear people say, "I shouldn't care what others think," or "I am stupid to care about what they think." I see many similar quotes on Facebook. And while the sentiment is an indicator of striving for self-fulfillment, it might make some of us even more self-critical. My answer to that is, of course we care what others think. Our belonging is contingent upon what others think. It matters to us as social beings who need to belong in order to live.

The ego has the role of ensuring that we do belong and protecting our social status. The threat of not belonging sets the ego in motion one way or the other, and how it chooses to respond is often based on past history and experiences. Rejection is a huge threat, and the ego will respond by seeking a solution to rejection. How we compensate for rejection is often to find ways to not be rejected again. We may find a new group to belong to—maybe renegades. We may try to convince ourselves that we don't need to belong and then dive into counterproductive behaviors (finding belonging in electronics, drugs, our work, etc.).

If we don't accept that we are social animals with a need to belong, we will react unconsciously and our choices will not serve us. Rejection, abandonment, and betrayal are all social fears. These things strike us to the core and wound us deeply. They engage our fear system on all levels, mental, emotional, and physical. How does it help us to reject ourselves again for needing to belong? In truth, that is what we do when we criticize our human need to belong. Let me tell you how this has impacted me.

I learned from a young age that I was supposed to be selfless, kind, and giving. The message was do not seek attention for yourself. Do not seek approval. Do not be conceited or seek status in any form, for that means you are a bad, shallow person. Unfortunately, I bought into these messages wholesale. I could not accept that I had a need for attention, and so could not see that my ego had attached itself to the status of being a perfectly selfless female. I was wounded over and over again by rejection. I looked for other places to belong. I sought out renegades like me and pretended that I didn't care what others thought. Meanwhile, I felt like I was dying inside, totally unworthy and ashamed. As we have discussed, shame, unprocessed and unspoken, becomes toxic and leads to all kinds of unhealthy behaviors. At least I belonged somewhere, however. I belonged with my family and I belonged with the other renegades. But I always secretly (even from myself) wanted to belong in those groups where I was rejected. I set about to proving to them that I was worthy, and imagined that one day I could reject them in return, and then they would be sorry.

Seeking fame is the ultimate in unconscious-rejection reaction. I wanted fame to prove I was worthy, but I wouldn't consciously allow myself that desire. Unconsciously, that desire drove everything I did for a time, until I became aware of it, anyway. Once I accepted it and saw it for what it was (compensation for the pain and shame of not being good enough to belong), it ceased to completely take over my life. What also complicated the matter was my very real, deep desire to share my wisdom and support others in their growth, and to do that I had to become more public. In order to put myself out there, it was vitally important to heal this tangle created by the ego to compensate for rejection. Otherwise, the rejection that would inevitably come with being more public would be devastating to that Little Girl who wanted to be loved and cherished for who she was.

When we accept that we have a deep-seated need to belong, that it is a matter of life and death for us and that the ego is working to protect us, then we have the power to choose. We aren't acting out to compensate. When we can allow ourselves to experience the very real grief we feel from our experiences of rejection, betrayal, and abandonment, and approach ourselves with compassion—when we can do that, we begin to heal. Self-love and understanding come from knowing how we are made, what it means to be human, and accepting that there is a purpose to the way we are made. The ego, like fear, is not our enemy. It is part of who we are. The ego is our social fear system, and like our physical fear system, we need to understand it in order to work with it.

Bring the light of your conscious awareness to the ego and you are empowered to make the best choices for yourself. It is like choosing to walk through your fear of rejection, to try again and again if need be, and to love and accept yourself and your courage for doing so. It is a common cultural experience for us to try to be other than what we are in order to fit in. It takes great courage to risk being ourselves when it goes against the norms of our tribe.

The Worry Brain

Another part of the fear system that is not talked about much is the planning part, which happens in the prefrontal cortex. Our thinking brain helps us plan for future dangers, providing protection through planning. Let's call this the "worry brain." If we think ahead, we can avoid dangers and prepare for potential disasters to ensure survival when faced with the different kinds of dangers in our world. There are the physical dangers, such as tigers, rock slides, falls, earthquakes, violence from other humans, etc, and there are also social dangers. As we are social animals and survive in groups, we have our tribal mind. Being part of the tribe, belonging and status are part of our survival. The ego helps us regulate our sense of belonging and place in our tribe. Higher status makes for more pleasure. Rewards come in both physical and psychological form. Our egos like to be rewarded. I want to emphasize that this is all normal. Sometimes, when we are too identified, we may constantly compare ourselves to others and never feel like we are good enough. Soon we can get bogged down in investing all our energy into our status. These days, status comes in many forms. In some groups, as I suggested earlier, status is gained by being more of a victim; in others it is defined by how much or how little we have. Take a moment to think about how often you compare yourself to others, and around how many different things? Can you observe this pattern without judgment?

I have a purpose for grounding fear and ego as a normal part of human development. I do this so that you can forgive yourself for being human. It is important to understand and accept rather than demonize parts of ourselves. Acceptance and awareness give us a range of choices and responses that are more realistic, whereas avoidance and creating shadows just shoves them more deeply under the surface where they fester and interfere deceptively. I know this well, as illustrated by the stories I have stared about myself. Now I want to address some ways that fear shows up. From my own experience I have categorized three types of fear: Core Fears, Future Fears, and Avoidance Fears.

Core Fears

Core fears come from an experience, typically during our childhood, that embeds a belief about ourselves. Often we spend our lives working unconsciously to overcome this belief, while remaining unaware of how it is driving our perspective about ourselves and impacting our behavior. Typically these beliefs come with shame. Core beliefs may have been something we were told by peers, parents, or teachers, or they could be rooted in how we responded to events that occurred. They persist in the background of our awareness, such that we cannot counter them with new evidence to the contrary. Core beliefs are likely no longer true to our character, but because they exist without our awareness, persisting on some level, and we respond as if they are still relevant. In order to counteract core beliefs, they need to be brought into the light of awareness. This way we can consciously choose to let them go and free ourselves from their hold. I have confronted several of these in my journey, and it amazes me how they can remain present underneath my awareness, and how freeing it is to finally confront them and let them go. I will share an example.

When I was in grade school, my best friend lived across the street and I often went over to her house to play. She had a brother who was a year younger and he was a bully. He loved to pick on me. I was easy prey because I was rather passive due to other circumstances in my life, one of those being my religious education, which taught me to be "nice" and "turn the other cheek." Now, let me say that these things were also tied to a core value for me, which has been true all my life, and that is a value for kindness. However, kindness does not have to show up as defenselessness. But that was how my childhood mind understood it. There were other issues that played a role here too, other past experiences for which I felt great shame, and that shame played a role in my response to being bullied.

At any rate, one day I was over at my friend's house when her brother started picking on me. I used a submissive strategy to avoid conflict, but that just provoked him more and he proceeded to punch me in the stomach. I caved in and started to cry. My friend stepped in to defend me and punched her brother back. I don't remember what happened immediately after that. All I remember now is that I felt defenseless and ashamed of being unable to defend myself, and from that moment, I started to believe that I didn't have the strength or capacity to do so. As I compared myself to my friends and acquaintances, it seemed I was singularly incapable of standing up to people. I didn't have good verbal retorts to taunting and I wasn't comfortable physically defending myself. I saw myself as lacking courage, although I was a child, so I didn't have those words. I knew I was lacking something vital. I thought there was something wrong with me. There were several other experiences stretching into adolescence that validated this belief and drove it deeper into my core. Eventually, it went underground as I made my way into high school, college, and adult life.

What is interesting is that I also had experiences, particularly in high school, where I started to fight back. In fact, I confronted a well-known bully from the football team. When I think about this incident now, I was full of both courage and spunk. He said something terribly rude to me and I retorted skillfully and slapped him across the face, then stomped off, leaving him stunned. But incidents like that didn't count against my core belief about being incapable of defending myself, as it was so embedded under the surface. As long as I was unaware of it, I could not counter it. Flash forward to 2012, when I went to a workshop to learn to facilitate training in a job connections group I had joined. The training was not at all what I expected. Once the facilitator introduced himself, he began by telling us we were all meant to be there because circumstances had conspired to bring us together. Next he asked us why we were there. A gentleman sitting next to me answered, "Because I want to learn to facilitate workshops." The facilitator responded with, "And what will that do for you?" The gentleman answered, "Then I will learn a new skill." Once again, the facilitator asked, "And what will that do for you?" The gentleman answered, "I will be able to put the new skill on my resume." And so this line of question and response continued. The facilitator kept digging with the same question and the gentleman went deeper and deeper into his reasons.

I sat there next to him, both listening and answering the questions for myself, going deeper and deeper into my reasons. Eventually, I got to a point where the real answer emerged. I was there because I was afraid I was going to let myself down, *again*, at which point I burst out crying. The facilitator turned to me and asked, "What's happening?" I responded, "I am afraid I am going to let myself down." He asked, "Why do you think you will let yourself down?" Suddenly, the image of being punched in the stomach by my friend's brother surfaced into my awareness. I haltingly told the story to the facilitator and my classmates, and burst into tears again. They listened and supported me with kind words and compassion. In fact, everyone applauded my courage for being so vulnerable in the classroom.

There was a man from Africa, I don't remember which country, but he said that he was inspired by my vulnerability. He said, "You help me feel more hopeful about Americans because sometimes I wonder if there is any feeling and authenticity here at all." This gave me a new perspective about myself and courage. In the next moment, I could see the many times I had stood up for myself over the years and confronted the belief with a new reality. With that armor, I was able to silence that particular inner critic. From that point on, whenever that specific inner criticism came up again, I had new awareness and information to counter it. In the following three years, several situations arose where I might have caved and given my power away on an even more intense level than I had experienced before, but I stood up for myself in each. It was as if I was being tested. I passed these tests with spirit and spunk. Once I became aware of the core belief, it no longer had the power to control me. I could combat it with a list of the times when I had stood up for myself, which helped me realize I didn't lack courage and grit after all. With this new sense of capability, I was able to face these intense situations where that belief might have caused me to cave. I may not have responded perfectly to each situation. I may have gotten defensive, made assumptions, and fumbled through it (I am human, after all). But the most important piece *for me* was that I took a strong stand for me. Doing it "perfectly" ceased to matter. Doing it "perfectly" harkened back to my training around being nice. Sometimes nice and accommodating are the opposite of what is called for. Sometimes anger is what is called for, and I got angry! All my training around accommodation went out the door in these situations, and each time I gained more appreciation for my ability to stand up for what is right for me. This core belief no longer holds me back. I hope my story illustrates for you the concept and potential impact of Core Fears. Now let's discuss how to uncover them.

As you saw in my example, one way to uncover Core Fears is to keep asking powerful questions. This is one of the primary tools in coaching and facilitation. A good question can lead us to deeper places within ourselves. Sometimes just diving into what a word means *for us* can lead to new insights. Paying attention to the images and memories that arise can be a big clue to the origin of a core fear. If you have the image, you can examine what happened and the things that were said. It's very important to set aside judgment as you do this, and to be curious. Remember, when we are children we do not have the same capacity to understand motives or examine beliefs. You must support your inner child in this process and care for him or her in a reassuring and nurturing way. I often encourage my clients to visualize their inner child and hold and comfort them. I use visualizations to get to the core belief as well. I don't think this is territory easily tread alone. It can help tremendously to have a compassionate observer and skilled questioner. In my story lies the whole thrust of how core fears work and how to move beyond them.

How to Process Core Fears

- **Step One: Identify the Fear.** The first step in dealing with core fears is to identify them, bring them into the light of your consciousness, and see them for what they are: a reaction or compensation for an experience we had in the past. In my case, there were several times that I was bullied in my childhood, so it wasn't just one event, but a string of events that led me to believe I was incapable of standing up for myself.

- **Step Two: Bring Compassion.** The second step (and this is so important) is to bring compassion to your inner child. In my case, once I remembered the experience, I had compassion for that frightened and shamed little girl. I also experienced the compassion of the other classmates and the facilitator, which helped me to be more compassionate toward myself. With the help of the facilitator, I uncovered the reasons (the "turn-your-other-cheek" lesson) for my response to the situation and I loved that little girl as if I were her mother. We can be so much harder on ourselves than we are on others. My shame was a judgment. Letting go of it allowed me to grieve for that sweet little girl who wanted to do the right thing. I allowed myself to experience that grief and release it through tears.

- **Step Three: Counter the Fear.** The third step is to counter the fears. The past is never a true indicator of our future, and we can always find positive stories to counter the validity of the core belief. We have a choice. Even if we have a hard time identifying positive stories, we can change. Bringing compassion to the situation already changes it. In fact, current research indicates self-compassion is one of the markers for those who recover from PTSD.[18] Nevertheless, the positive stories help, because they redirect the habitual neural pathways where the fear or belief was embedded.

I highly recommend finding a healer who can help you with these steps. A good healer can guide you through the steps, and more importantly, can help you surface the core beliefs so you can work with them.

Future Fears

Future fears are stories we create about what is going to happen in the future. The fodder for these stories is the past and is often related to our emotional triggers. There may be a probability for things to occur, but what we know about the future will always be nothing more than speculation. Personally, I don't believe in future predictions, and as you have already read, I don't find it terribly useful to know the future. In fact, physicists question whether time is real. Change or movement is synonymous with conceptual time, which gives rise to the notion of past and future. We generate the perception of time

---

18 Buczynski, Ruth. N.D. "Self-Compassion: The Secret to Reducing PTSD Symptoms." Accessed May 11, 2018. https://nicabm.com/self-compassion-the-secret-to-reducing-ptsd-symptoms-2/

through the observation of change. Change can be stressful. We like to be comfortable and the unknown forces us to adapt, to step outside our comfort zone. Add that to our negative, sticky minds, and contemplating the future tends to be an exercise in fear of change.

It is human to fear change even though we cannot do much about the future anyway. The best we can do is plan for potential hazards of the future, such as earthquakes, storms, and upcoming seasons by preparing just-in-case food supplies, practicing drills and evacuation plans, and setting aside an emergency fund. Beyond that, we cannot do anything except cultivate peace of mind and skills to cope with disasters and loss. As I suggested before, our worry brain tends to believe that enough worrying may magically forestall events. In fact, if we worry too much we are not present with what is happening right now, and it wastes our energy. So, how do we put our worry brain to rest?

How to Process Future Fears

- **Step One: Become Aware.** The first step is to recognize when your worry brain is in control, and then stop it. You can recognize the pattern when specific words show up in your inner vocabulary like "if," "then" or "I'm never" or "always." Other clues are that the stories can't possibly be verified. In other words, they haven't happened to you.

- **Step Two: Ask Yourself "Is it True?"** Byron Katie suggests asking yourself, "Is this true?" And again, "Is this Absolutely true?" If the answer is no, it's probably not real, is a form of catastrophizing, and is a waste of your time.

- **Step Three: Be Present in Your Body.** To stop your worry brain, bring your awareness to the present moment and to your body, your sensations. I have never found a better strategy for stopping my negative inner dialogue than just becoming as present as possible in the moment. Your thinking brain cannot take up the same space as presence.

- **Step Four: Express Gratitude.** An excellent follow-up strategy to counter the negativity is to find things to be grateful for. Do this practice every day. Get specific with it. If you are trying to accomplish a goal, find things related to that goal to be grateful for. This will train your brain to track the positive and is a good counter for negativity.

Avoidance Fears

Avoidance fears are really just plain old denial. We are terrified of looking at reality. Shame and fear often go hand in hand here. The best example I can think of from my own life is related to financial issues. At one point, my husband and I were so much in debt, I avoided looking at it and determining the total amount of money we owed. The fear of that number was so great that I paid the minimum amount due every month on my credit cards without ever looking at the total, and I certainly never put it all together. The denial was in place to protect me from the shame I assumed I was going to face if I looked at the total. But what occurred was that I was scared all the time. I was so ashamed that I couldn't even look at the total, because as long as I was in denial, I never really knew what I was faced with, and my mind was free to make up things and make it worse. The more I avoided, the more fearful I became until it got to the point that I just didn't even want to be here anymore. I couldn't do anything about the debt because I didn't know what it was, so I couldn't come up with a reasonable strategy to work with it. And so it hung over my life like a big black cloud, day after day. I was miserable.

I finally found the courage to look at it. The first thing that I did was talk to a financial therapist, who held space for me to confront the shame and shift my beliefs about money and my ability to manage it. Avoidance fears come from our belief that we are not going to be able to cope with the reality. We are afraid of our emotional response. This is also one reason why I put such emphasis in this book on emotional awareness and being in the body. We are far more capable than we give ourselves credit for. Here it is useful to look again at the stories we are telling ourselves about the situation. In my case, I was telling myself I was a total failure with money. The financial therapist was able to help me see that my money story was inherited from my family, had to do with cultural mythology about what it means to have money problems, and that it was possible to create a plan to make it better.

Processing Avoidance Fears

- **Step One: Acknowledge the Issue.** Start by acknowledging the issue (denial never works). Reality is typically less scary than what we imagine. In my experience, finally facing the truth was a relief.

- **Step Two: Seek Help, If Necessary.** Determine whether you need help and seek it out. It helps to have a trained professional or a nonjudgmental friend to help you not only look at the issue, but work through the shame. Use the tool of experiencing the emotion in the body and processing it.

- **Step Three: Make It Manageable.** Break the issue down into components. What we have been avoiding often feels overwhelming and too big to deal with. When we break it down into components, it begins to feel more manageable.

- **Step Four: Develop a Plan of Action.** Create action plans to address each component. This makes it so much easier to follow. Each action you take is movement forward, and that feels good.

- **Step Five: Work Your Plan.** Stay focused and work through your action plan, and reward yourself appropriately, even if it's just a simple acknowledgment of your courage. Find a way to track your steps and the results. This is a good way to remind yourself that you are making progress.

Moving Through the Ego and Fear to Wisdom

Given that fear and ego can go into overdrive and create both emotional and physical health issues, one thing I want to stress is the wisdom of our bodies. It doesn't work to try to override our bodies, despite the fact that we have been raised to do this in Western culture with its emphasis on transcendence. The body is our "brain"—it is our navigation tool, our pleasure center, and our soul's vehicle for learning and growth. We incarnated for a reason, and it wasn't an accident. The Judeo-Christian myth of The Fall is so often presented as a transgression and a mistake, but it actually had purpose and was part of the plan. Our bodies are a gift and present the means by which the soul can learn what it needs to learn while incarnated, for however many times.

It is important to trust your body, and also be alert for when it moves out of balance. Developing intuition is a combination of combining the wisdom of our bodies with the wisdom of our spirit and soul. The answers are available if we know how to access them, and that takes some learning around how to manage ego and fear. Often the ego's desire for status, while completely human, can get in the way of our ability to listen to the wisdom of our soul. Sometimes we just have to make mistakes to learn. Our growth, however, requires that we eventually learn to listen to the wisdom of the soul and the divine guidance that comes from deep within us. I am speaking of tuning into our trunk and being aware of our roots that reach to the eternal center of Being.

So, how does one learn to manage ego and fear? It starts with being present and aware. On page sixteen, I gave a Presence Awareness Meditation. The more you practice becoming present in this moment, the more you become aware of everything, including the ego with all its stories about your life. You become more aware of your emotions and their ephemeral nature, and you build resilience around discomfort. Presence awareness is the key to all these things, and it is also the start to being more aware of your intuition. The more

you become quiet in your mind, the more you strengthen
your roots.

One truth about fear is that sometimes we just have to
move through it. Some fear is truly a warning, but most of our
fears are nothing more than a passage. If you are not moving
through your fears, then you may not understand the reality
of this. Avoidance only serves to shrink our comfort zone and
increase our fear. It can be exhilarating once you reach the
other side of fear.

I have another story from life to illustrate. Late one day my
husband and I decided to go for a hike. There was not much
daylight left, but we decided to go anyway. We went to an open
space we favor, which has many trails that wind up through
the hills and ridgelines. These hills offer wonderful vistas of
Northern California—open savannah interspersed with dark-
green patches of oak, bay, and buckeye, or sage and manzanita
scrub. The trail we wanted to hike winds its way up onto the
ridge, over the humps, and eventually leads to a steep canyon
created by a creek carving its way downward. A thick canopy of
trees lines both sides of the creek, which joins a larger creek at
the bottom in a lush valley between two ridges where the trail
joins the main route back to the parking lot.

It was a wonderful hike, but our estimate of the time it
would take to execute it was off. We hiked up to the ridge, and
at the halfway point to the canyon trail, the sun was already
making its way down the horizon. When we finally reached the
canyon trail, it was dusk. There was still visibility on the ridge
but as we entered the steep incline, we plunged into darkness. I
could barely see where I was placing my feet. Having hiked this
way many times, I was familiar with the shear wall and depth
of the drop-off bordering the left side of the trail. One misstep
would mean a serious fall and could be deadly. Trembling, I
carefully placed each step, ensuring that my foot was on solid
ground before transferring my weight, thinking it was going
to take us a long time to get down to the main trail. With each
step I took, my terror notched up another level, gripping my
gut, raising my heartbeat, and shortening my breath. Slowly,

we crept down the trail. Finally, the ground leveled out and spread beneath our feet, creating room to step sideways safely. I paused and took a long, deep breath, relieved. I felt the rush of exhilaration. My skin tingled as I felt the blood coursing through my arteries. Elated, I gushed, "That was intense!" It had been a journey through fear and we both had conquered it. In that moment, I knew I was capable of pushing through the resistance that fear erects, but I was resilient, strong, and proud of myself. In fact, to this day I don't think I have felt as alive as I felt in that moment.

The other side of fear is a very different feeling, and this story illustrates it on a visceral level. Fear is a visceral thing. Even when the fear is all in your head, your body still responds. You cannot know the other side of fear until you pass through it, but once you do, it is electrifying and rewarding. However, we often let our fear persuade us that we are capable of much less than we are. Before entering that trail, my partner and I almost turned around to go back the way we came, but then decided to go for it. Of course, there was no guarantee of safety. There never is; safety is an illusion. At any moment in time death, loss, or harm can take us. But we convince ourselves that if we take the safe route in life, we will live longer, avoid trouble, and be happier. Safe isn't what we are here for, otherwise life would be safe. It is not. We know and understand this in our gut. When we choose safe, we dim a little bit of our soul. Our wildness wants adventure, and what is adventure without danger? We never know our mettle without passing through risk and fear.

That brings me to what lies on the other side of fear. When you work with your fear consciously, when you listen to it and apply discernment, and use some of the tools I shared with you, asking it questions, being present with the body, and processing your emotions, then you empower yourself. Sometimes it is important to listen to your fear and to protect yourself. But both your growth and transformation require moving through your fear. It takes courage to make ourselves vulnerable, and to risk our potential and eventual loss—for we will lose. Loss in life is a given. But we will never succeed if we don't try.

Moving through our fear is also the work of loving ourselves deep enough to answer the call of our soul. This is the classic Hero's Journey story as identified by Joseph Campbell. Part of our soul's task is accepting that grief is always a possibility, knowing that the deeper we love, the deeper our grief will be when what we love is lost. It is incredibly courageous to choose love because grief always lies on the other side of love. When we choose love, we inevitably choose not to let our fear get in the way of life. To love is to walk through fear. The hero/heroine makes a sacrifice. Her heart is sacrificed to and for love. From that comes deep compassion for the human condition and all humans. This is the choice of a human fully conscious and aware. This is our spiritual work. Our soul calls us forward into love, growth, and wholeness. At the same time it calls us into being exactly who we are, accepting our unique gifts and our purpose, even when it goes against the norm. When we love ourselves, we make that possible, and when we make that choice we call *our* tribe, the right tribe for us.

The crucible of fear is the alchemical vessel that has the power to transform us into gold if we approach it with awareness and choose to move through it. Here is what is on the other side of fear in my experience:

- **Full experience of the life force:** I experience this when I face fears of physical barriers and bodily harm (for example, diving off the high board for the first time). Terror can sometimes enliven us, like it did for me after hiking down that steep trail in the dark. Terror can remind us exactly how alive we are, and that is invigorating. There is a reason some people become risk junkies, a reason why we seek out thrills.

- **Sense of accomplishment:** Knowing that I did it, I met the challenge, survived it, and expanded my comfort zone. It shows me my mettle and builds my confidence. I am capable of far more than I imagined in my fear-lined mind. Each time I walk through a fear, I become more.

- **Awareness of my worth:** I am aware of my strength, and I earn deeper trust in my wisdom and increase my sense of self-worth.

- **The knowing that all is well:** I know I am resilient, that I can bear loss, and that I will rebound. I can use the wisdom gained from experiencing loss to serve others on an even deeper level.

- **Gratitude:** I am grateful for the grace given me to survive, grateful for being alive, grateful for more time to cherish what I love.

These things are worth far more than the security on the safe side of fear. And of course, the truth is, we are never truly safe from loss or death. That is an illusion. To walk through fear is to choose to live, to be alive.

Fear is the Guardian at the Gate

Every mystery tradition from around the world understands this truth: to die before you die is the ultimate passage through and beyond fear and into life. I have experienced this in little ways. I wish those mystery traditions were still alive. The Eleusinian Mysteries are just one example. It is said that those who went through these mysteries faced death and found life. Here is a quote from Pindar about the mysteries: "Blessed is he who has seen these things before he goes beneath the earth; for he understands the end of mortal life, and the beginning (of a new life) given of God" (Pindar Fragment 102).

What does that mean, to die before you die? To die before you die means to strip away all the structures that the ego is identified with that make you rigid; to let go of all you know and to step into the unknown and into mystery. In the cycle of myths about Inanna, the myth about her descent to the underworld describes her journey.[19] As she descends, she faces seven gates, and at each one she is stripped of all her regalia, all those things that represent her power in the world of form. You could say these things were the emblems of her identity.

When you die before you die, it means you realize that at the core of you is only awareness. Everything else is just ever-changing form. As Eckhart Tolle says, "Existence is the foreground of life; Being is the background."[20] We get trapped by our obsession with form and ignore the background. To become aware of Being, look at the space between things rather than the things themselves. Listen for the silence that holds sound, and you will begin to become aware of the background. It is subtle. It does not demand our mind's attention like form. The only thing that never changes is the awareness that is you, which is also the whole of Being, the Divine. To face your fear of dying is to let go of all you know and receive the mystery of awareness. The ultimate unknown is death, and the ultimate fear is the fear of death, which is really a fear of the unknown. When faced with the unknown, we are stripped of everything we think we know. We cannot pass through the gate until we are stripped of our fear. Fear stands at the gate and asks us to pass through it to reach the other side, and to do so we also must let go of all our ideas of who we are and embrace mystery. This is the ultimate transformation into a life that is led by awareness rather than definition, which to me is the ultimate in intuition. Not many of us will reach this state in our lifetime, but we can take the journey.

What is the other side of fear like for you? How will you cultivate awareness and work with the ego? What choices will you make in order to deepen your intuition?

---

19 Wolkstein, Diane. 1983. *Inanna, Queen of Heaven and Earth: Her Stories and Hymns from Sumer.* New York: Harper Perennial.
20 Tolle, Eckhart. 2005. *A New Earth: Awakening to Your Life's Purpose.* Penguin Books, p. 220.

SECTION III

BUILDING YOUR INTUITIVE MUSCLE

CHAPTER SEVEN

DEVELOPING A RELATIONSHIP WITH INTUITION

So far in this book, we have explored what gets in the way of intuition, and how to manage fear, emotions, and ego. Now let's circle back to the beginning of the book, back to the theme of awareness, and focus again on developing your intuitive abilities. That is, after all, the result you were most likely looking for when you decided to pick up this book.

Your intuition is your own. It may be similar to mine, or completely different. Either way, it is yours and is unique to you. No one else can tell teach you its nuances, which means you have to spend time getting to know it and developing a relationship with it. Like any relationship, it can be a bumpy road sometimes. But this relationship is well worth the effort, and will be the most rewarding relationship in your life. Whenever we develop relationships, we build trust, and that takes time. Trust has to be earned. Trust goes both ways. As you begin to develop a sense of trust in your intuition, in return it opens to you, trusting you to listen and revealing more as you do.

I can't emphasize enough how vital trust can be to a good relationship with your intuition. Like any other relationship, trust maintains connection. When we don't have trust, we create walls. Without trust we cannot connect. In my experience, intuition only works when we learn to trust it. That is a high order in a world that denies the reality of our inner world and actively works to tear down our self-trust. After all, we won't buy and spend addictively if we trust ourselves and our intuition, or find answers inside ourselves. When we trust ourselves, we have little need for experts to tell us what we need or how we are wrong and how we can "fix" ourselves. Then we are not so easy to manipulate.

Our culture relies on manipulation and coercion and has done so for thousands of years because it has largely been a culture of domination. Yes, our culture is changing and you are part of that change, especially since you have read this book. Trusting yourself and your intuition is the key to your freedom. It doesn't mean doubt won't creep in. Sometimes doubt plays a vital role in deepening our faith by cracking open the hardened shells of our identity and the ego, so it can be a good thing. However, that is different from a pernicious ongoing self-doubt that erodes our sense of worth and our ability to align with our inner wisdom. With that in mind, I suggest that you think of your intuition as your intimate partner and approach developing your healthy relationship with it as such. For whatever reason, we tend to be much more respectful and careful with others, especially at the beginning of a relationship, than we are toward ourselves.

Curiosity has been a theme in my other books and I want to bring it in here too. Curiosity is a wonderful tool for developing relationships. Curiosity removes judgment, calms expectations, and opens us up to experience wonder over what we are curious about. Approaching your intuition with a spirit of curiosity will help you learn how your intuition works and how it best serves you on a much deeper level.

I generally don't like self-help books that give prescriptions or step-by-step instructions. They tend to bore me because I don't believe one method works for everyone, but I do think that some guidance will be useful here in a general way. If you want to build your relationship with your intuition, there are steps you can take to help. My personal opinion is that the best step you can take to develop your intuitive abilities is to build your presence awareness by bringing yourself present as often as you can. Go back to the Presence Awareness Meditation near the beginning of this book and make it part of your daily practice. Throughout your day, when you remember, surrender your senses to what is present, even while you are working or conversing. You will be amazed by how you are able to be both present and focused at the same time. However, be patient with yourself. It is normal to get lost in your thoughts as you practice this skill. When you notice you have gotten lost in thought, gently nudge yourself back. You will find that you move in and out of awareness. It takes time and intention to build awareness for longer periods of time, and more often. You will get better as you practice. Presence awareness is the key to how I got where I am today.

A Journaling Exercise to Cultivate Intuition

Building awareness will only help and will never hinder your progress. Below are suggestions for how to build your relationship with your intuition. It's good to start by asking yourself some questions for clarity, to ferret out some of your expectations, and create some specific intentions.

- **What is it you really want out of this relationship with your intuition?** What are you hoping it will do for you?

- **What is your intention for cultivating intuition?** (Do you want to deepen your relationship with yourself or some person, to trust more, to experiment, to play? Do you want to start with using intuition for fun stuff, work stuff, home life, all life?)

- **Is it fair what you are asking of your intuition at this point in your relationship?**

- **What commitment are you willing to make? How will you follow through with that commitment?** Will you use daily divination tools, meditate, pay attention to your body, practice with friends, and/or notice your inner pictures, inner dialogue, feelings, and sensations? You can use Chapter Two on the Clairs here to come up with ideas.

- **How will you track your progress in developing your relationship?** Will you use journaling, artwork, collage, notes on your smart phone, or some other method?

- **What will you do to acknowledge progress?** Perhaps tell a friend, tell your coach, celebrate, or reward yourself.

Take some time to think about and journal your answers. Now put yourself in your intuition's shoes. How would you, as an intimate partner, respond to those expectations?

A Visualization for Enhancing Intuition: Meet Your Inner Tree Knower

Next, get curious and find out more about what your intuition desires. It will help to do visualization, and in it, meet with Intuition. Here is a guide for the visualization and some questions to ask in your meeting:

Find a comfortable, quiet spot where you can relax and be uninterrupted. Close your eyes and begin by becoming aware of your breath. Next, notice where there is tension in your body. Breathe into the area of tension, and when you exhale, let it go. Imagine it flowing down your legs and into the ground. After your body is relaxed, allow yourself to drop into your inner world. Once there, find yourself walking down a trail with a sense of anticipation. You are headed for your favorite tree. Notice the sights and sounds along the way. You arrive at the border of your special tree and pause to take a look at it. Notice the texture of its trunk, notice how broad it is and how tall. Notice its shape. Locate a spot to settle in, lean against your tree and make yourself comfortable. Now allow yourself to merge into the tree and find yourself in a vast inner cave filled with the light of stars. You find yourself brimming with anticipation again, because you know your inner tree knower—your personal guide—is coming to meet you here. In fact, you see your guide walking toward you now. As your guide walks toward you, notice how it looks and sounds. Greet it like a long-lost friend. Thank it for coming to meet with you and then ask the following questions:

- What shall I call you (name)?

- What do I need to know about you? What do you know about me?

- What is the best way for me to listen to you? What do you want or need from me?

- What are the next steps for building a stronger relationship?

- How can I talk to you when I need to?

Now it is time for this meeting to come to a close. Thank your inner tree knower and say goodbye for now, knowing that you can talk to them anytime you want.

After the visualization, write down notes about what transpired. Don't second-guess the answers that come up. Begin building your trust today! See what emerges after this exercise. How does it change how you feel about your intuition?

You may want to revisit this exercise every once in a while as things shift. As we learn and grow, our intentions and commitments change. Come up with your own questions. What do you want to ask?

Allow Your Awareness to Continue Expanding

The next step is to continue to expand your awareness. Start practicing being aware of your internal experience. You may not know what your cues mean, but you will never know if you don't pay attention to them. Sometimes these cues can be very subtle; other times we've disregarded them to such a degree that we totally ignore the information. Be patient with yourself. It takes time to make the shift in your awareness. We have minds made to distract us with an ongoing stream of storytelling and internal dialogue. Here's an example from my interaction with trees of what happens when we practice noticing and honoring internal cues.

A number of years ago, I set the intention to interact and communicate with trees. My expectation was simple: I was curious to see what would happen if I tried, and of course, I was hoping that they would communicate back. I made a commitment to spend time with trees every time I went hiking or for a walk, and to simply place my hands on their trunks and notice what came into my inner vision as well as what I felt energetically. At first all I noticed was the feeling of the bark and the breeze on my face. I silently said hello, thanked the trees, and moved on. After a while I began to notice that as I placed my palms on the trunks, there was an energy pulling me toward where the trunk split. I felt that energy in my groin. It was subtle, but it was like a tug. Soon after I experienced this tug, the thought came into my mind that the heart of the tree must be right before it split into branches. It was not long after this that I had the experience with the golden streams of energy and the coyotes, which I shared earlier.

My sensations are sometimes followed by *knowing*, but not always. My job is simple: just notice. All of this also requires managing the ego and its expectations. I notice that when I want something profound to happen, I am less able to be present to what is actually happening. Most trees I have approached have felt welcoming. In some cases, I sensed great love emanating from them. I felt warm, my heart expanded, and my eyes filled with tears of joy. I have only approached one tree where I felt energetically repelled. It was like a push. I placed my hands on the trunk anyway. It was subtle, but unpleasant, because it was a bit like being pushed in the gut and had a buzzy energy. I apologized and stepped away.

Being aware is the key to noticing your intuition, especially when it is speaking in a subtle voice, which it often does. When you are distracted by your inner dialogue, that subtle voice gets lost. Becoming aware changed my life. I began to appreciate the present moment more and more, for the calm it brought in my life, for stopping the endless cravings for something different, for finally experiencing Divine Presence in my life. I pause, I listen, I am guided. You can have this too. It's not only my special power, it is also yours. I am not the only voice out there saying this either; pick up a book by Eckhart Tolle or Joe Dispenza and you will find the same message about expanding your awareness in the now.

Friendships and Intuition

It's wonderful when your awareness can be confirmed, and friendship plays a vital role in that. I speak with trusted friends about my experiences and also have the opportunity to listen to theirs. I belong to a small circle of women who meet eight times per year for ritual. We have been meeting for over twelve years. During that time we have shared our deepest fears, our greatest joys, our losses, and much laughter. Over the years the trust has deepened to a level where we can truly let go and go deep in our rituals, as there is no fear of judgment if things get a little unusual—and they do at times. We have become experts at following the energy together. Trust, the freedom to experiment, and a no-dogma approach helps immensely.

The reason I bring up these friends is because I owe so much of my own intuitive growth to our relationship. They have affirmed my experience so often. After rituals we have shared our internal experiences with each other, and often have found that we were experiencing many of the same feelings and information, if not exactly in the same form.

One time several years ago, we met at my house for our gathering and parked ourselves under one of the trees in my backyard. We usually do a check-in, where each of us gets to share what is happening in our lives. We shared food and decided to draw Tarot cards, which at this point had become almost obligatory for every meeting. I remember feeling bored during the card reading, but I didn't say anything. Later, we shared some follow-up emails. One sister shared how the card reading had felt "excruciating." A flurry of emails followed. In that string of emails we all learned how the card reading felt "off" in one way or another—my boredom, her excruciation, another's restlessness. We had all overridden our internal cues during the ritual. The sharing helped us to validate our experience and know that energetically we were tuning into something deeper than each of us.

It was profound to share this way. From it, we learned to speak up. We deepened our trust in one another and our ability to understand how the energies might be communicating with us. We came to a consensus that nothing had to be obligatory, and we committed to being more attuned to the energy. We speak up sooner now when things feel off. Every once in a while we get into a rut, but it is group-corrected through our shared commitment. Sometimes it is not comfortable, sometimes it is incredibly vulnerable, but we continue to grow as a circle, and I continue to grow as an individual inside this circle of women.

My relationship with my circle has increased my inner trust exponentially. We all need support along our journey. Do you have friends or trusted mentors with whom you can share your inner experiences, without fear of disbelief or judgment? Can you experiment and try new things together, and then share about what happened for you both internally? This can be a wonderful way to build your intuitive muscles and trust your inner senses.

Using Your Intuition and Awareness
To Navigate The Outer World

We have spent most of this book looking at the innerverse of inner awareness, emotion, body, fear, and ego. Now we will shift into applying the wisdom that comes from inner awareness to navigating through this world of material incarnation. This is the playground for your soul. The outer world is a mirror for your soul and the schoolyard for our growth.

Nature reflects back what is sacred inside us. To be in nature is often a space for the soul's respite. It is where we touch into the sacred more easily. It is easier to tap in when out in nature, as nature naturally causes us to pause and reflect; however, we tend to think of nature as being out in the woods or the wilderness. In fact, nature is also all around us and we are nature.

Signs and synchronicities can show up in our technology too. The key is we have to pay attention and have the right mindset. Most of the time we are in a trance, a mind-induced, habitual trance. As we have learned, cultivating presence awareness helps us overcome that trance. For some reason it is easier to remember to do this out in nature. Our world of electronics tends to induce a deeper trance, but that does not mean we can't be conscious with our electronics too. In fact, it is a good practice to approach them with awareness, observe how they suck us in, and then choose to not get caught up in them.

The Gift of Nature

Once upon a time we felt more deeply connected to nature. Nature is magic. But somewhere along the way we shifted and began to see nature as something to conquer and control. I believe that the concept of ownership was a major cause of this shift that led to so much environmental destruction. With ownership came the loss of our sense of connection with nature as sacred, and we moved our sacred places inside, into

Come my friend, she says
Sit by this Being you call tree

Lean in
Allow yourself to melt into me
and become one
with the grass beneath your feet
Come my friend, she says
Enter into
This Bliss

Whoosh, rock doves fly in pattern against the crystalline sky,
opening ears, opening eye
Haunting cries pierce the air, puncture my heart,
My throat longs to answer, to also take part
Larnyx pushing upwards, I open my lips,
Silence ensues, throat fixed by bliss
As tears of joy grace my face, One by one,
coyotes trot by, six in a pace

Come my friend, she says
Sit by me, this Being you call Tree
For if you come, Here, Now,
The world answers your fervent plea
You Are already at One

We Are
This Is
Eternal

~Maura McCarley Torkildson

churches and synagogues. Of course, many of those mimic nature and, as evidenced by elaborate stained-glass windows, we bring nature themes inside our buildings. Most of the nature religions were destroyed or co-opted into Catholicism as imperialism spread from Europe to the far parts of the world. Pagan religions are relegated to "primitive" corners of our religious history, while the monotheistic religions are upheld and revered. Of course, nature is still a source of inspiration and themes of nature wind their way through our literature, architecture, art, poetry, and religious texts. While nature inspires us, still we seek to fully tame and control it, just as we seek to tame our inner wild. Culturally, we find it hard to accept mysteries unsolved. Our science is led by an ethos that often feels aligned with Francis Bacon's statement to "torture the very secrets from nature," a statement born of the very time that science began to assert itself over religion, but still aligned with a world view of dominance.

We can learn something from those so-called "primitive" religions. They understand signs and synchronicities as messages; their devotees have honed their abilities to read them. As quoted by Zitkala-Sa (Sioux writer and activist): "A wee child toddling in a wonder world, I prefer to their dogma my excursions into the natural gardens where the voice of the Great Spirit is heard in the twittering of bird, the rippling of mighty waters, and the sweet breathing of flowers. If this is Paganism, then at present, at least, I am a Pagan."[21]

Holding reverence for all life, rather than owning it and asserting power over it, leads to a deeper connection. And from Luther Standing Bear: "It was good for the skin to touch the earth, and the old people liked to remove their moccasins and walk with bare feet on the sacred earth … the old Indian still sits upon the earth instead of propping himself up and away from its life-giving forces. For him, to sit or lie upon the ground is to be able to think more deeply and to feel more keenly. He can see more clearly into the

21 Zitkaka-Sa. Accessed May 11, 2018. http://www.azquotes.com/author/23043-Zitkala_Sa

mysteries of life and come closer in kinship to other lives about him."[22]

What we "own" becomes a burden, a weight that occupies our mind space in such a way that it shifts our perception into a need to control and "protect" what we own from "others" as well as from nature (i.e., the natural forces that change everything, such as aging, erosion, floods, etc.). It leads to jealousy, covetousness, and feelings of lack. It is a downward spiral from there, taking over our minds and bodies so that everything becomes mundane. Ownership makes mystery problematic, rather than a source of awe and wonder. It causes us to lose our curiosity and replace it with avarice. Think about it...how much of your fear is about losing what you have? How does that fear in particular take up space in your mind, causing you to forget to be in wonder and awe about what is present in this very moment? How much of your mind is preoccupied with keeping what you have or getting more, or comparing what you have to what others have? I know this can take up a lot of space in my mind, as I too am a result of this culture of materialism in which we exist.

The Wisdom of Insecurity

The concept of ownership is a trance, a mass-induced trance that keeps the wheels of this machine churning endlessly and takes us far from our true inheritance—our connection with the spirit of life unfolding, the Great Mystery. Ownership is fear manifest, an offshoot of insecurity. We "own" things for our security, to have and to hold. Ownership (beyond what we truly need in order to live) is not the wise response to fear. It is giving in to it. At its worst, ownership leads to slavery. Keep in mind that insecurity is all about the fear of future loss.

Here's another quote from Standing Bear, a wise response to insecurity: "The old Lakota was wise. He knew that a man's

22 Luther Standing Bear. 2006. Land of the Spotted Eagle, New Edition. Lincoln: Bison Books.

heart, away from nature, becomes hard; he knew that lack of respect for growing, living things soon led to lack of respect for humans, too. So he kept his children close to nature's softening influence."[23]

If approached with awareness, loss softens us. To accept loss as inevitable is to grow up, to become adult. Otherwise we act like children, throwing tantrums at the world for not having things "our way," and we cannot mitigate grief wisely when we do not accept loss as part of life. How different would our lives be if we accepted loss as inevitable, if we allowed it to open our hearts rather than seeing it as just a tragedy. To accept loss is to be open.

How much of your mental space is occupied by the burden of your stuff? How much of your day to day activities revolve around ownership? What is your relationship to nature? Don't approach these questions from a dogmatic point of right or wrong, but rather by what is the right balance for you? Are you getting enough nature in your life? What lessons can nature teach you about true security and belonging?

Signs and Synchronicities

Signs and synchronicities (meaningful coincidences) show up all over the place. All it takes is for us to pay attention. For whatever reason, this has become difficult for most of us. We live in a noisy world with many demands and a distracted mind that constantly pulls us away from presence awareness. Letting go isn't something our minds do well. The word *surrender* has become synonymous with defeat and submission. However, to become aware of the signs and synchronicities all around us, we need to be able to surrender. It requires a certain openness. Signs often show up where we least expect them, and if we slow down, we just might notice them. It is also important not to assign meaning right away. When we force meaning, that is the mind and ego taking over and taking control. Meaning

23 Ibid. p. 197.

needs to arise naturally, as if it comes from someplace else (which it does).

Here is an example of synchronicity in my own life. I was meditating one morning in the easy chair in my living room. My cat Avatar was nestled on the blanket on my lap, purring softly. My hands tenderly draped over her body and I could feel the vibration of her purr under my fingers and palms. The sweet pulsation of her love crept up my arms and into my heart. I swelled with gratitude for her. Suddenly, I became aware that my father was there in the room with me. It's hard to explain how I knew; I just did. The knowing arose from deep within my being. As I surrendered to my knowing, I became aware of another presence there with him. This presence felt like it was behind him, holding him, and from it came an intense but gentle light radiating outward. Riveted by awe, I sat in stillness and my inner voice said, "Dad, you're with Jesus."

As the feeling subsided, I didn't want to leave the moment behind. I sat quite still, in reverence, for some time. To move felt like blasphemy. The moment needed its due and my total presence in order to properly honor what had just occurred. Eventually, it became clear that I needed to move into my tasks for the day, so I clasped Avatar in my arms and kissed her head before placing her on the floor and making my way to my office. I sat down, grasped the mouse, and glanced at the computer monitor. Facebook was on my screen and for some reason it was blown up large, so that someone's post took up the whole screen. All I could see was a picture of a black square that contained white block-letter words. I couldn't see who posted it, nor could I see any of the typical comments posted below. The message in the words was this: *God has just opened a door for you that no one can close.* Mouse in hand, thinking, *That is weird,* I nearly began scrolling down the screen in my habitual manner to see what else was going on, but then I stopped myself. *What are you doing? This is a message for you. Pay attention! This is punctuation for what you just experienced!* I paused, expanding my earlier moment of gratitude in a silent prayer: *Thank you, Universe, thank you.*

I was very aware in this Facebook moment of how I nearly bypassed this punctuation on my experience, with its clear message of validation. That validation was asking me to trust my senses and my experience. *Yes, this is real. Trust what you feel!* I suppose the enlarged size of my page could be explained. I probably did it myself unknowingly. I've done it before and since. Facebook also has a way of automatically updating, so that I am no longer on the post I was last viewing. All of it could be explained rationally, but that does not discount my experience.

We insist on living with an either/or perspective, somehow needing to prove our experience away into reasonable, mundane little slices of life. Why are we intent on dissolving meaning into mundanity? We ridicule other cultures for their superstitions, refusing to see our own. We cling to science to help us explain the mystery of the world away, leaving it barren of magic, and us smug with our cleverness. Instead of using science as a tool to increase our awe, we wield it as a weapon and worship on the altar of proof. I need no proof for what I felt and understood. All I needed was to simply trust myself and my experience. I have room for both science and mystery, times where proof may be necessary and times when I can just trust my inner knowing. All is possible. I enlarged the screen by accident, Facebook updated to this post, AND it was incredibly meaningful for me, however it got there. How it got there matters less than what it meant for me.

This is synchronicity, and I am profoundly grateful for the grace that stopped my hand and the awareness that allowed me to pause, to pay attention, and to give that moment the gravity it deserved. In many ways it's so simple. Pay attention. Allow yourself the experience through your sensation and through your emotion. Emotions are not your enemy. Sensation is not a distraction. We have these gifts to help us navigate through this manifest plane in which we experience both life and our divinity. If we pay attention, signs and synchronicities show up all over the place.

So what is the difference between delusion and meaningful coincidence? How do we untangle that deceptive web? I look at the world around me and see it rife with delusion. I have my own delusions. We all do. Delusion is the province of the ego and of impatience. We want answers now. We want results that fit into our stories and make us comfortable. But comfort and bliss are not in the same arena. Comfortable is limiting. Bliss is expansive. Bliss can also be overwhelming. Our bodies and egos may respond to bliss with fear, and contract. Have you ever contracted when confronted with expansive bliss? Allowing ourselves to experience bliss may be too painful, because we will miss it sorely when it passes. That is the logic of fear. *What if I never feel this again? What if I don't deserve it and it is taken away? What if it's not real? What if I am just crazy?*

I've been on that edge. I can feel my own limits to my ability to experience bliss. It is a muscle that we have to stretch and grow. Bliss so often comes only through grace. We may never experience it again in the same way. But we must ask ourselves, is it better never to experience it at all, or experience it even just once? Personally, I will take it even just once rather than not at all. This life, on this manifest plane, is about experience, it is about love, and it is about loss too. Life is ephemeral and so is everything in it. Everything comes and everything goes. What we have, what we feel, what we love, and what we experience will arise and it will dissolve. The ego desires permanence, comfort, and safety. In order to get these things, we create the illusion of control. Control even appears to work for a period of time. We can control objects, data, our emotions, people, or even nature for some time. However, all things will always move beyond our control.

We can drive ourselves crazy trying to control. We can become increasingly manipulative, destructive and parasitic, leeching the life force from everything around us if we let the hunger for control get the better of us. We can create the delusion that we can be all-powerful, that we know everything, and we twist our experience to fit into the mold we have created with our minds, often trying to force round pegs into square holes, torturing the round pegs as we do so. Acceptance, gratitude, curiosity, and awe, these are full of reverent humility—the opposite of arrogance. They are not about control. Humility is elegant, grounded, and non-possessive. These qualities are aligned with love. *Love* is the Whole. Love includes grief in its embracing arms. Delusion accepts nothing. Delusion has no curiosity. It has one goal and that goal is usually grandiose, puffy, and bloated. It is actually repulsive, but the desire for control and our projections may attract us toward grandiosity.

Grandiosity is like the campy sideshow to humble awe. It may trick us into believing it is real for some time, but it will never feel expansive. The energy of grandiosity is contracting, restrictive. It substitutes tinsel to capture the light. But tinsel only reflects the light, it never contains it. In order to contain light, we have to become a vessel that accepts darkness as the contrast that allows the light to truly shine. Light contains shadow, just as shadow contains light. They are intimately woven together and accepting of each other. They embrace in loving union—a union of opposites. Both light and shadow cannot be controlled or captured. Light travels at its own speed, and darkness contains stillness. They both have their own laws. Perhaps this was why Albert Einstein was so fascinated by light his entire life.

The first step to becoming aware of signs and synchronicities is to be present for them. As I have suggested many times already, practice presence awareness. This hones your ability to notice what is present. The second step is to observe what arises within your awareness. Third, notice how your body is responding. Are you filled up? How do you know when something is meaningful for you? Define your physical sensations of meaning. I can tell you mine, and I have throughout this book as examples, but it is important that you know what those signals are for *you*. They could be very different from mine. The final step is trust. I think this can be the hardest step of all. All our lives we have been trained to seek answers outside ourselves. Part of that is because we are social beings, but mostly it is because we live in a culture that does not encourage inner experience and seeks to control our experience at every turn. It is a huge step to trust yourself, especially when the messages that arise counter the prevailing assumptions about reality. If you find it hard to trust yourself, ask these questions:

1. What does my body tell me about my experience? Is it contracting or expanding?

2. What is the worst thing that could happen if I believed my experience was real?

3. How would having others believe my experience change it, or not?

4. What voice inside me is telling me this can't be real? Is it my own, or does it sound like a particular person from my life? What is the purpose of that voice? (Ask it.)

Trusting yourself takes time. And yes, it does help to have someone to validate your experience just by listening and accepting what you have to say. Someone who can ask the right questions to help you deepen your knowing about your experience is even better. It is necessary to have a willingness to be vulnerable enough to share your intimate inner experiences, and that courage attracts to you a trusted friend or mentor who can listen, be supportive, and who accepts who you are. I have been lucky enough to have many of these kinds of people in my life. Their support enabled me to grow into the person I am today. It is good to remember that since reality can be incredibly deceptive, it is helpful to have guides along the way. I have been fortunate to have those as well. These were people in my life who challenged the status quo and my beliefs, but in ways that held me with love. When we are ready, the universe supports our growth by placing those guides in our lives.

Trust also comes from experimentation. Validation comes from testing and tracking results. As I described earlier, in my coaching certification program we were encouraged to blurt our intuitive impressions without censoring them. In addition, we were encouraged not to be worried about being right or wrong—to just throw the thought out there and see how it lands. If it doesn't land, so what? No big deal. Just move on. I am repeating it here to underscore the importance of this because when we take the risk and don't worry about being right, a huge sense of freedom comes, allowing us to play and learn. When we need something to be right, our need for being right gets in the way and we start prejudging everything we say. And nothing restricts the creative flow more than judgment and censorship. When we worry about being right, we contract and become wound into a tight little ball that allows noting to enter.

What is the worst thing that can happen if your impressions are "wrong"? The worst thing could be that you learn something vital that leads you to the bull's eye of the target, and there is nothing "bad" about that, no matter how uncomfortable. It is only our inner judge that makes it into something bad—a reason to tell you that you are worthless or a screw-up. Don't believe it. It's not true. You just did an experiment and you learned. That is a step forward. In my experience, even those "wrong" moments have sometimes turned out to be right in the end; it just took the person I shared them with a while to come around to what was shared. And how do we know that what we share isn't just what the receiver needed to push back against, to further clarify what they needed to understand? I have seen it work that way too. The universe works in mysterious ways and we don't usually have the whole picture.

Developing Relationships with Trees and Nature

Here is what I do when I'm out on a hike. I open up my senses to what is present, feeling the breeze on my face, listening to all the various sounds, sensing my feet on the ground, taking in the temperature, and looking around. What captures my attention? Movement garners my attention and I am particularly aware of birds, being a long-time bird watcher. But sometimes the light hits a particular leaf on the ground, throwing up a splash of color; or the skyline bends into a pleasing curve or dramatic angles that lead my eye; or a scent wafts into my nostrils, begging me to inhale deeper. It can be incredibly calming and joyful to be immersed in these landscapes that fill my senses. I take it all in with my awareness.

As I walk along, I notice trees. One usually stands out in some way. It may be the way it leans, or it could be the sheer mass of its trunk. Sometimes it is the pattern of lichen or moss on its bark. And then I experiment. I approach the tree and I say hello. Often I ask for permission to touch it. How do I know if I have permission? I close my eyes and ask myself, *What do I feel?* Sometimes I can feel an energy pushing against me. I take that as resistance, a "no." Other times I feel welcome; it feels loose and easy inside my torso and I approach, gently placing my palms on the tree. So often in the past I have been compelled to put my hands on the trunks of trees, but did so unconsciously. It wasn't until the day I asked myself, "I wonder what would happen if I just paid attention to what happens inside me when I place my palms against the trunk of this tree?" I didn't have expectations. I was just curious as to what would happen, and I was observantly aware. Since I didn't have any big expectations, I was able to observe even the most subtle sensations.

It's funny how having no expectations creates all kinds of freedom to notice what is there. My body is a finely tuned vessel. When my mind is bent toward letting go into awareness, it becomes aligned with my body rather than fighting or directing it. This opens vistas. The first time I did this was quite amazing. What I noticed was that I suddenly had a vision of the bark in my inner eye, as if I were moving along just above the surface of the bark, like an insect in flight. I called it binocular vision, because it felt like I was looking at the trunk through binoculars. I had no idea what it meant, and didn't try to create a meaning out of it. I just accepted it and thought it was fun. I was learning. That was impetus enough to keep doing it. It did not occur to me until later that I was seeing with my third eye. I love learning this way, having the experience and finally receiving the insight as it percolates up from somewhere deep inside me. It's a bit like a treasure hunt; I never know what I am going to find, and that excites me. This way, the ego is circumvented and I can just receive and learn.

As I have practiced, my awareness grows deeper into more and more subtle aspects of my experience. Things I was previously unaware of now come into my attention. Sometimes I like to call them doorways inside my being. They may have been closed before, and hidden from my awareness, but as I pay attention I keep finding new ways to see and feel. Inside I have this knowing that those things were always available to me, I just didn't know how to see them or be aware of them. It is a process of building awareness to new levels all the time. One thing that has always been hard for me is patience, but I am finally getting a handle on this. The process doesn't happen in an instant, and now I can be patient with it, love the journey and the discovery, and relax into it. If I feel my impatience knocking at my door, I breathe, bring my awareness back to my sensations, and surrender. I trust that my sharing this resonates with you.

Sometimes I like to capture my experience one way or another, whether that is writing about it, making a note on my voice memo, or creatively expressing it through art. Being so present to my experience creates deep grooves in my being. Some things stay with me for years and eventually come through in my creative outlets one way or another. My book *The Curious Magic of Buckeye Groves* was like that, and so was an altar cloth I made recently. The altar was inspired by sycamore trees in Oak Creek Canyon in Arizona, from my travels over fifteen years ago. When I am truly present in my awareness to an experience, it never leaves me and I trust that. I don't have to worry about saving it somehow, through pictures (they never capture the whole anyway) or through writing about it immediately. That doesn't mean it is wrong to write or photograph; just realize that your presence is all that is really needed and the experience will never leave you and may even grow of its own accord.

Experiences can be like seeds, and it is important to nurture them without bringing them into the light immediately. These things have their own tides. We learn this over time, and we also learn to build that trust. Don't worry too much about the accuracy of memory. A quote by Damon Galgut, like so many quotes about memory, says: "Memory is fiction.... All memory is a way of reconstructing the past. The act of narrating a memory is the act of creating fiction."[24] To me this means that all moments are subsumed into the now. Reality is timeless movement, shifts in our perception. Our memories are about us and our growth, redefining who we are as we grow.

Can you put yourself in a curiosity mindset and bring yourself to presence awareness when you are out in nature? Move toward what captures your attention and approach mindfully, aware of what is happening inside and out. Try not to "make something out of it" right away. Just be in the experience. Be patient. Watch how it evolves.

Using Oracles

All that I have covered thus far in this book prepares you to use oracles. I started this book with the intent to create a companion book to go along with a tree oracle deck I am creating. The book decided to get written first, and evolved into what it has become. It still serves as a companion for reading oracles, but in a much different way than I had originally imagined. As I dove in, I realized how important it was to cover all the things that get in our intuitive way. After all, reading oracles is all about listening, seeing, and feeling with that intuitive sense. The more you become aware, inside and out, and the more you set judgment aside and cultivate your curiosity, the more you open yourself to your intuition. Oracles come from nature, from the computer screen, from a message from a friend. Oracles are synchronicities. They can show up anywhere, anyhow. The trouble is, we often don't take the time to pay attention or give them significance. We are in a trance most of the time, lost somewhere in our minds.

Pema Chödrön has said that our minds need to be trained. They do what they naturally do—think—but we have to train them to be aware. This requires guiding the mind back to a

---

24 "Damon Galgut Talks About His Novel *In a Strange Room.*" 2010. Accessed May 11, 2018. https://www.theguardian.com/books/audio/2010/sep/07/booker-prize-shortlist-damon-galgut

relaxed state of awareness, over and over again. One way to look at the mind is to see it as just another sense. Knock it down off the pedestal it has been on in the West. The Vedics thought of the mind in this way and there is a lot of wisdom in that. It opens new possibilities of being.

If you desire to begin working with an oracle deck, my suggestion is to approach with patience and experiment. Don't get caught up in being right or wrong. Read for your friends in an atmosphere of play; in other words, don't take it too seriously. Personally, I think it is really hard to do a reading for yourself. I have so much more freedom when I read for others. I am not so emotionally tied up in others as I am in myself, especially when I want something to be a certain way, or when I am dealing with my fears. So, when reading for myself, I usually don't ask big questions with a lot riding on them. That is a prescription for shutting down my intuition. Often what I do for myself is pull a card asking about the energy of the moment and feel into that. I look at the picture and create a story about what the character is doing. What do their eyes tell me? What comes up about the scenery? What is happening? What is being carried out by the characters? Then I ask, how might that apply to this moment for me? What can I learn from what this card is showing me? If I find I start to spin off into mental acrobatics or my gut clenches (a fear response), I remember that the card is not a prescription. I can set it down and leave it alone, and come back to it later.

I pulled the Honesty card (in my Fairy Oracle deck) a few days before this writing. I reacted with a bit of fear. I asked myself, *What am I not being honest with myself about?* My gut wrenched a little. I breathed and gave thanks, then put the card down, realizing that I needed to be patient and allow the meaning to evolve. Throughout the day I kept going back, asking, What do you want to tell me? This enabled me to relax around it. The card was about what is not working in my life. I already knew the answer, but was feeling confused and sad. The truth was I just needed to experience the grief I was feeling about things not working out the way I wanted them to. Until

I worked through the emotion, I was in no place to receive answers. Allowing the grief to be expressed softened me, opening me up. I worked with this card for days, allowing the emotions to be present, and allowing myself to experience the physical expression of them. It pointed to honesty on a deep level—right where I was emotionally in such a grounded, real (if raw) place, allowing me to navigate step by step.

There is movement, and movement is good. So often the mind wants to make it into a big deal. Then of course, being a "big deal," it is overwhelming and then I can't deal. So what am I trying to say here? Beware of reading for yourself. Beware of the mind, ego, and fear taking over and making a big deal out of it. Approach it with curiosity, ask little questions, ease your way in. Read for friends as often as you can and see what happens. You will learn, you will begin to trust, and you will get better at it. If it is something you want to do and you are committed to it, your skill will evolve. The more you practice, the better you will get.

I also draw a card for a teleconference call I offer weekly. When I pull the card I find a part of the image that stands out to me. That is my way in, and as I start to speak about it I end up riffing and am often surprised by what comes out of my mouth. I let it flow and it's just fun. Trusting myself, not worrying about what others think, gives me the freedom to be in the flow. Sometimes these readings are pretty profound. The more risks I take to go into the passion and feeling, the better the reading. At times I have found myself in ecstatic tears.

I have tried many decks over the years and have discovered that some resonate and some don't. I quickly stop using the ones that don't resonate or speak to me. It is important to find oracles that resonate for you. Perhaps for you it will be runes, or reading tea leaves, or using a more traditional deck. Don't be afraid to try things out, all the while being aware of all the signals arising from your body—that finely tuned, amazing instrument with which you navigate through this world. Most of all, trust your body and your own intrinsic wisdom to lead you down the right path.

CONCLUSION

It has been a journey writing this book. I have been evolving as I have been writing, and that is both wonderful and a challenge. As I keep adding new learning, I can see how I could never be done with this book. Like a tree, I shed my leaves and grow new ones, my branches reach higher and bow lower, and my roots take up more nourishment. At some point we have to choose to complete a project, and so it is with this book, even though there will always be more to add.

I am convinced that we have reached a quickening. I can feel it within myself. My intuition keeps expanding, as does my trust in myself. I wish the same for you. I hope you have found my insights, examples, and musings helpful by way of example rather than prescription. I invite you to visit my website www.mauratorkildsoncoaching.com to sign up for my complimentary Presence Awareness meditation and find out more about upcoming offerings. You can also connect with me on Facebook: www.facebook.com/MauraTorkildsonCoaching/

May the tree that you are tremble with meaning and joy as you move deeper into your own presence.

ACKNOWLEDGMENTS

Where does one to start to thank people for influencing and supporting a book, both directly and indirectly? There are so many people who have influenced and supported me over the years. If you've touched my life, you have probably influenced this work. However, I will start by acknowledging my father. You can see in this book that he had great influence on my life, even in his death. My father was a tree admirer and lover of nature, so I learned that from a great source. My father wasn't perfect. Like me, he grew and changed over his lifetime, becoming ever more compassionate and wise as he got older, and I learned from watching him. In many ways we grew together. My mother has had great influence, and her caring stands out. She loves deeply, and especially loves her children; that love is a gift she gives to all beings in her life. Many of my childhood friends liked to spend time at our house because of the caring, love, and safety that existed in my home. My mother is also endlessly curious and what a joy to have received that trait myself. Thank you, Mom!

I am fortunate to have a loving family with a sense of humor. Laughter was present in our home and that has been a life saver for me. It wasn't that I didn't experience any trauma—we all do—not one person does this life perfectly. But my family has grown along with me and the very basis of my family experience was love, caring and humor. My sisters, Kyanne and Tonia, and my brother, Carl, you were there with me; we learned from each other as we grew up and still do. Together we form a family bound by love, humor, humility and meaning.

My husband, Peter, is a continual font of support (and laughter) and my daughter, Megan O'Connor, has been one of my greatest teachers in life. I am so proud of who she has become after facing some painful challenges in her youth. She is a constant reminder for me of human strength and resilience.

Certain people I met later in life have been on this path with me and have had great impact. I am so grateful for my dear friend Marguerite Rigolioso, founder of Seven Sisters Mystery School, who has been on this esoteric and entrepreneurial journey with me. I have sometimes leaned on her heavily as I worked through putting myself and this topic out there into the world. She has been a supporter, an activator, a teacher and an amazing friend. Her courage inspires me; her intelligence amazes me; and her willingness to be herself and be vulnerable gives me hope for seeding an emerging world that has more magic, more compassion, more depth.

My women's circle, Sandra Vaughn, Karla Donohue and Viola Lew Simcox, have been with me on this journey for even longer. I have learned so much together with them as we explored life, intuition, magic, and relationships in our circles and beyond. I am grateful for their ongoing influence and love.

Next there are those who more directly supported this work. I will start with Cris Wanzer of Manuscripts to Go who edited this book and my novel, *The Curious Magic of Buckeye Groves*. She ensured I had clean manuscript to pass along to my publisher. Writing is a process of revision and more revision and she has helped me become a better writer both grammatically and content wise.

As I was in the process of revising *The Inner Tree,* I met Randy Fauver at a talk he gave and proceeded to become a great admirer of his work. I couldn't have asked for a better Foreword for this book. I love how he blends science and intuition and I am incredibly grateful not only to have his wisdom and knowledge included herein, but also to have him in my life as a friend.

I feel very fortunate to have found Penelope Love and Citrine Publishing for publishing this book. Thank you, Chloe Rachel Gallaway, author of *The Soulful Child*, for suggesting Citrine Publishing! Penelope has lovingly shepherded this book to publication. I intuitively knew she was the right publisher in our first conversation, but have come to appreciate her commitment, diligence, skill, artistry, and wisdom over the time we have worked together. In addition, I want to thank Rolf Busch for his beautiful cover and how he incorporated my artwork into a beautiful design that captures the essence of this book so powerfully.

My writing group—Ana Maria Galvan, Charles Burke, and Cecilia Pugh—fostered this book along, especially in the early part of writing it. Their weekly dedication and feedback were enormously helpful and kept me on track with my writing. My writing teacher, Janice De Jesus, inspired this group and she helped me to become a much better writer and even to see myself as someone who could publish books. She did that for many of her students.

My clients continue to be a source of great inspiration. Their willingness and courage to dive deep into sometimes painful places in order to grow is the best hope of all for me. I adore creating a safe space for that exploration to occur and I am frequently amazed by their wisdom and capacity.

Brené Brown is also a great influence, even though I don't know her personally. Reading her books has taught me so much about myself and what it means to be human.

I need to mention my post-graduate education too. I received my Master's Degree in Women's Spirituality from a combination of programs: California Institute of Integral Studies (CIIS) and New College of California. I learned an alternative way to look at culture and spirituality in those programs. However, it was my training at Coaches Training Institute (coactive.com) that brought many of the concepts to life for me and served me to put them into action in my life. I had an excellent Life Coach to support me in the certification process in Gina Paigen. She was a huge part of my successful completion of that program. All the teachers in that program, as well as my personal coach, Gina, have much to do with the content of this book.

I want to specifically thank Rose Wognum Frances, my first teacher in the CIIS Women's Spirituality Program. She exemplifies the intuitive artist, role modeling how trusting you inner inspiration can create amazing things, be they books, artwork or other expressions of the soul. Her multidimensional art carries incredible depth, beauty, and meaning. I remember the first time I heard her speak, she wove a spellbinding story of her experience in the redwood trees, sharing how the magic of redwoods' resilience, embodied in the ring of new trees that grow around the stump of a logged tree, offered real hope echoed in the resilience of the Divine Feminine and women. This story has continued to inspire me to this day.

I have been lucky enough to participate in California Reentry Institute, founded and led by Collette Carroll, who deserves a mention here, too. Collette's incredible work and compassion have created an amazing opportunity for prisoners at San Quentin to transform and become who they were always meant to be as contributing members of society. I am grateful to her for the way she role-models the impact of compassion and for her invitation into the prison to work with the prisoners in her program. This opportunity allowed me to see the powerful results of some of the concepts presented in this book in action. The men in that program are more proof that we should never give up on people and I am grateful for them.

To all my other friends and teachers I have met along this journey, I am grateful to you as well, for showing up, for being you, for being vulnerable, for your unique wisdom. My universe continues to expand, and if you have interacted with me, you have enhanced my life and influenced the work here and beyond. Nobody does this kind of work alone. The concept of ownership does not represent reality and so many people, probably even unrecognized by me, have lent something to this work.

Readers, thank you for choosing to read this book. You were the inspiration that kept me writing. I wrote it for you.

Finally, to all the trees that have shared their majestic strength, ability to foster life, gravity-defying magic, and palpable love, I love you. You are truly the wisest among all beings. Your ongoing presence and lessons nourish me. Thank you Universe, for being the most amazing tree of all, which I am fortunate to be part of and which includes Everything that IS.

REFERENCES

Armour, J. Andrew. 1991. "Intrinsic cardiac neurons." *Journal of Cardiovascular Electrophysiology* 2 (4):331-341. doi: 10.1111/j.1540-8167.1991.tb01330.x.

Armour, J. Andrew. 1999. "Myocardial ischaemia and the cardiac nervous system." *Cardiovascular Research* 41 (1):41-54. doi: 10.1016/s0008-6363(98)00252-1.

Armour, J. Andrew, and Jeffrey L. Ardell, eds. 1994. *Neurocardiology.* New York, NY: Oxford University Press.

Atari, N. A. 1982. "Piezoluminescence phenomenon." *Physics Letters A* 90 (1):93-96. doi: 10.1016/0375-9601(82)90060-3.

Atchley, Ruth Ann, David L Strayer, and Paul Atchley. 2012. "Creativity in the wild: Improving creative reasoning through immersion in natural settings." *PloS one* 7 (12):e51474. doi: 10.1371/journal.pone.0051474.

Baconnier, Simon, Sidney B. Lang, Maria Polomska, Bozena Hilczer, Garry Berkovic, and Guilia Meshulam. 2002. "Calcite microcrystals in the pineal gland of the human brain: First physical and chemical studies." *Bioelectromagnetics* 23 (7):488-495. doi: 10.1002/bem.10053.

Barrett, Lisa Feldman, Karen S Quigley, Eliza Bliss-Moreau, and Keith R Aronson. 2004. "Interoceptive sensitivity and self-reports of emotional experience." *Journal of Personality and Social Psychology* 87 (5):684-697. doi: 10.1037/0022-3514.87.5.684.

Bassler, Bonnie. 2001. Tiny conspiracies: Cell-to-cell communication allows bacteria to coordinate their activity. *Natural History* 110: 16-22.

Beauregard, Mario, Gary E Schwartz, Lisa Miller, Larry Dossey, Alexander Moreira-Almeida, Marilyn Schlitz, Rupert Sheldrake, and Charles Tart. 2014. "Manifesto for a Post-Materialist Science." *EXPLORE: The Journal of Science and Healing* 10 (5):272-274. doi: 10.1016/j.explore.2014.06.008.

Becker, Robert O., and Gary Selden. 1985. *The body electric: Electromagnetism and the foundation of life.* New York, NY: Quill.

Berker, Ennis, Gary Goldstein, John Lorber, and Betty Priestley. 1992. "Reciprocal neurological developments of twins discordant for hydrocephalus." Developmental Medicine & Child Neurology 34 (7):623-632. doi: 10.1111/j.1469-8749.1992.tb11493.x.

Berman, Marc G., John Jonides, and Stephen Kaplan. 2008. "The cognitive benefits of interacting with nature." *Psychological Science* 19 (12):1207-1212. doi: 10.1111/j.1467-9280.2008.02225.x.

Bierman, D. J., and H. S. Scholte. 2002. "Anomalous anticipatory brain activation preceding exposure of emotional and neutral pictures." Toward a Science of Consciousness Conference IV, Tucson, AZ.

Bohm, David. 1980. *Wholeness and the implicate order.* New York, NY: Routledge.

Bohr, Niels. 1934. *Atomic theory and the description of nature.* Cambridge, England: Cambridge University Press.

Brymer, Eric, Thomas F. Cuddihy, and Vinathe Sharma-Brymer. 2010. "The role of nature-based experiences in the development and maintenance of wellness." *Asia-Pacific Journal of Health, Sport and Physical Education* 1 (2):21-27. doi: 10.1080/18377122.2010.9730328.

Burrill, Devin R., and Pamela A. Silver. 2010. "Making cellular memories." *Cell* 140 (1):13-18. doi: 10.1016/j.cell.2009.12.034.

Cardeña, Etzel, John Palmer, and David Marcusson-Clavertz, eds. 2015. *Parapsychology: A handbook for the 21st century.* Jefferson, NC: McFarland.

Cardinali, Daniel Pedro. 2016. "The prescientific stage of the pineal gland." In *Ma vie en noir: Fifty years with melatonin and the stone of madness,* 9-21. Switzerland: Springer.

Christakis, Nicholas A., and James H. Fowler. 2013. "Social contagion theory: Examining dynamic social networks and human behavior." *Statistics in Medicine* 32 (4):556-577. doi: doi:10.1002/sim.5408.

Cifra, Michal, Eduard P. A. van Wijk, Heike Koch, Saskia Bosman, and Roeland van Wijk. 2007. "Spontaneous ultra-weak photon emission from human hands is time dependent." *Radioengineering* 16 (2):15-19.

Cleary, Thomas F. 2009. Vitality, energy, spirit: A Taoist sourcebook, Shambhala classics. Boston, MA: Shambhala.

Cocroft, Reginald B. 1999. Parent-offspring communication in response to predators in a subsocial treehopper (Hemiptera: Membracidae: Umbonia). *Ethology* 105: 553-568.

Dane, Erik, and Michael G. Pratt. 2007. "Exploring intuition and its role in managerial decision making." *Academy of Management Review* 32 (1):33-54. doi: 10.5465/amr.2007.23463682.

de Quincey, Christian. 2002. *Radical nature: Rediscovering the soul of matter.* Montpelier, VT: Invisible Cities Press.

de Saint-Exupéry, Antoine. 1944/1995. *The little prince.* Ware, England: Wordsworth.

Dijksterhuis, Ap, Maarten W. Bos, Loran F. Nordgren, and Rick B. van Baaren. 2006. "On making the right choice: The deliberation-without-attention effect." *Science* 311 (5763):1005-1007. doi: 10.1126/science.1121629.

Dunn, Barnaby D., Hannah C. Galton, Ruth Morgan, Davy Evans, Clare Oliver, Marcel Meyer, Rhodri Cusack, Andrew D. Lawrence, and Tim Dalgleish. 2010. "Listening to your heart: How interoception shapes emotion experience and intuitive decision making." *Psychological Science* 21 (12):1835-1844. doi: 10.1177/0956797610389191.

Eliade, Mircea. 1951/1964. *Shamanism: Archaic techniques of ecstasy.* Rev. and enl. ed. New York, NY: Princeton University Press.

Ford, B. Q., P. Lam, O. P. John, and I. B. Mauss. 2017. "The psychological health benefits of accepting negative emotions and thoughts: Laboratory, diary, and longitudinal evidence." *Journal of Personality and Social Psychology* Advance online publication. doi: 10.1037/pspp0000157.

Ford, John K. B. 1991. "Vocal traditions among resident killer whales (Orcinus orca) in coastal waters of British Columbia." *Canadian Journal of Zoology* 69 (6):1454-1483. doi: 10.1139/z91-206.

Friedman, Harris L., and Glenn Hartelius, eds. 2013. *The Wiley-Blackwell handbook of transpersonal psychology.* Malden, MA: Wiley-Blackwell.

Fukushima, Hirokata, Yuri Terasawa, and Satoshi Umeda. 2011. "Association between interoception and empathy: Evidence from heartbeat-evoked brain potential." *International Journal of Psychophysiology* 79 (2):259-265. doi: 10.1016/j.ijpsycho.2010.10.015.

Füstös, Jürgen, Klaus Gramann, Beate M. Herbert, and Olga Pollatos. 2013. "On the embodiment of emotion regulation: Interoceptive awareness facilitates reappraisal." *Social Cognitive and Affective Neuroscience* 8 (8):911-917. doi: 10.1093/scan/nss089.

Gershon, Michael D. 1998. *The second brain: The scientific basis of gut instinct and a groundbreaking new understanding of nervous disorders of the stomach and intestine.* New York, NY: HarperCollins.

Gigerenzer, Gerd. 2007. *Gut feelings: The intelligence of the unconscious.* New York, NY: Viking.

Gladwell, Malcolm. 2005. *Blink: The power of thinking without thinking.* New York, NY: Little, Brown.

Greenlaw, Peter, and Marco Ruggiero. 2015. *Your third brain: The revolutionary discovery to achieve optimum health.* Centennial, CO: Extraordinary Wellness Publishing.

Gross, James J, and Robert W Levenson. 1997. "Hiding feelings: The acute effects of inhibiting negative and positive emotion." *Journal of Abnormal Psychology* 106 (1):95-103. doi: 10.1037/0021-843X.106.1.95.

Gurwitsch, A. G. 1925. "The mitogenetic rays." *Botanical Gazette* 80:224-226.

Haluza, Daniela, Regina Schönbauer, and Renate Cervinka. 2014. "Green perspectives for public health: A narrative review on the physiological effects of experiencing outdoor nature." *International Journal of Environmental Research and Public Health* 11 (5):5445-5461. doi: 10.3390/ijerph110505445.

Henry, Richard Conn. 2005. "The mental universe." Nature 436 (7047):29. doi: 10.1038/436029a.

Herbert, Beate M., Olga Pollatos, and Rainer Schandry. 2007. "Interoceptive sensitivity and emotion processing: An EEG study." *International Journal of Psychophysiology* 65 (3):214-227. doi: 10.1016/j.ijpsycho.2007.04.007.

Hesse, Hermann. 1984. Bäume: Betrachtungen und gedichte. Berlin, Germany: Suhrkamp Verlag.

Hölldobler, Bert, and Edward O. Wilson. 2009. *The superorganism: The beauty, elegance, and strangeness of insect societies.* 1st ed. New York, NY: W.W. Norton.

Huxley, Aldous. 1945/2009. *The perennial philosophy.* New York, NY: Harper.

Ingerman, Sandra, and Henry Barnard Wesselman. 2010. *Awakening to the spirit world: The shamanic path of direct revelation.* Boulder, CO: Sounds True.

Ives, John A, Eduard PA van Wijk, Namuun Bat, Cindy Crawford, Avi Walter, Wayne B Jonas, Roeland van Wijk, and Jan van der Greef. 2014. "Ultraweak photon emission as a non-invasive health assessment: A systematic review." *PLoS One* 9 (2):e87401. doi: 10.1371/journal.pone.0087401.

King, Stephanie L., and Vincent M. Janik. 2013. "Bottlenose dolphins can use learned vocal labels to address each other." *Proceedings of the National Academy of Sciences* 110 (32):13216-13221. doi: 10.1073/pnas.1304459110.

Kingsley, Peter. 2003. *Reality*. Inverness, CA: The Golden Sufi Center, *Mahabharata* translation, p. 537.

Krippner, S. 2000. "The epistemology and technologies of shamanic states of consciousness." *Journal of Consciousness Studies* 7 (11-12):93-118.

Krishna, Gopi. 1995. *A kundalini catechism*. Darien, CT: Kundalini Research Foundation.

Lee, J., B. J. Park, Y. Tsunetsugu, T. Ohira, T. Kagawa, and Y. Miyazaki. 2011. "Effect of forest bathing on physiological and psychological responses in young Japanese male subjects." *Public Health* 125 (2):93-100. doi: 10.1016/j.puhe.2010.09.005.

Lewin, Roger. 1980. "Is your brain really necessary?" *Science* 210 (4475):1232-1234. doi: 10.1126/science.7434023.

Lopez-Munoz, F, and C Alamo. 2011. "Cartesian theories on the passions, the pineal gland and the pathogenesis of affective disorders: An early forerunner." *Psychological medicine* 41 (3):449-451. doi: 10.1017/S0033291710001637.

Low, Philip, Jaak Panksepp, Diana Reiss, David Edelman, Bruno Van Swinderen, and Christof Koch. 2012. "The Cambridge declaration on consciousness." Francis Crick Memorial Conference on Consciousness in Human and non-Human animals, Cambridge, England.

Maller, Cecily, Mardie Townsend, Anita Pryor, Peter Brown, and Lawrence St Leger. 2006. "Healthy nature healthy people: 'Contact with nature' as an upstream health promotion intervention for populations." *Health Promotion International* 21 (1):45-54. doi: 10.1093/heapro/dai032.

Marais, Eugène Nielen. 1937. *The soul of the white ant*. New York, NY: Dodd, Mead.

Marselle, Melissa R., Katherine N. Irvine, and Sara L. Warber. 2014. "Examining group walks in nature and multiple aspects of well-being: A large-scale study." *Ecopsychology* 6 (3):134-147. doi: 10.1089/eco.2014.0027.

Mayer, Emeran A. 2011. "Gut feelings: The emerging biology of gut–brain communication." *Nature Reviews Neuroscience* 12 (8):453-466. doi: 10.1038/nrn3071.

McCraty, Rollin, Mike Atkinson, and Raymond Trevor Bradley. 2004a. "Electrophysiological evidence of intuition: Part 1. The surprising role of the heart." *Journal of Alternative & Complementary Medicine* 10 (1):133-143. doi: 10.1089/107555304322849057.

McCraty, Rollin, Mike Atkinson, and Raymond Trevor Bradley. 2004b. "Electrophysiological evidence of intuition: Part 2. A system-wide process?" *Journal of Alternative & Complementary Medicine* 10 (2):325-336.

Merker, Bjorn. 2007. "Consciousness without a cerebral cortex: A challenge for neuroscience and medicine." *Behavioral and Brain Sciences* 30:63-134.

Miller, Melissa B., and Bonnie L. Bassler. 2001. "Quorum sensing in bacteria." *Annual Review of Microbiology* 55 (1):165-199. doi: 10.1146/annurev.micro.55.1.165.

Montgomery, Sy. 2015. *The soul of an octopus: A surprising exploration into the wonder of consciousness.* New York, NY: Atria Books.

Moore, Robert Y. 1995. "Neural control of the pineal gland." *Behavioural Brain Research* 73 (1):125-130. doi: 10.1016/0166-4328(96)00083-6.

Nisbet, Elizabeth K., John M. Zelenski, and Steven A. Murphy. 2011. "Happiness is in our nature: Exploring nature relatedness as a contributor to subjective well-being." *Journal of Happiness Studies* 12 (2):303-322. doi: 10.1007/s10902-010-9197-7.

Nummenmaa, Lauri, Enrico Glerean, Riitta Hari, and Jari K Hietanen. 2014. "Bodily maps of emotions." *Proceedings of the National Academy of Sciences* 111 (2):646-651. doi: 10.1073/pnas.1321664111.

Oschman, James L, and Maurie D Pressman. 2014. "An anatomical, biochemical, biophysical and quantum basis for the unconscious mind." *International Journal of Transpersonal Studies* 33 (1):77-96. doi: 10.24972/ijts.2014.33.1.77.

Park, Bum Jin, Yuko Tsunetsugu, Tamami Kasetani, Takahide Kagawa, and Yoshifumi Miyazaki. 2009. "The physiological effects of Shinrin-yoku (taking in the forest atmosphere or forest bathing): Evidence from field experiments in 24 forests across Japan." *Environmental Health and Preventive Medicine* 15 (1):18-26. doi: 10.1007/s12199-009-0086-9.

Pearsall, Paul. 1998. *The heart's code: Tapping the wisdom and power of our heart energy.* New York, NY: Broadway Books.

Pearsall, Paul, Gary ER Schwartz, and Linda GS Russek. 2000. "Changes in heart transplant recipients that parallel the personalities of their donors." *Integrative Medicine* 2 (2):65-72. doi: 10.1016/S1096-2190(00)00013-5.

Pepperberg, Irene M. 2000. "Possible levels of animal consciousness with reference to Grey Parrots (Psittacus erithacus)." *American Zoologist* 40 (6):893-901. doi: 10.1668/0003-1569(2000)040[0893:PLOACW]2.0.CO;2.

Pepperberg, Irene M. 2006. "Cognitive and communicative abilities of Grey Parrots." *Applied Animal Behaviour Science* 100 (1):77-86. doi: 10.1016/j.applanim.2006.04.005.

Pert, Candace B. 1999. *Molecules of emotion: The science behind mind-body medicine.* New York, NY: Simon & Schuster.

Pert, Candace B, Michael R Ruff, Richard J Weber, and Miles Herkenham. 1985. Neuropeptides and their receptors: A psychosomatic network. *The Journal of Immunology* 135 (2): 820s-826s.

Pollack, Gerald H. 2013. *The fourth phase of water: Beyond solid, liquid, and vapor.* Seattle, WA: Ebner & Sons.

Pollack, Gerald H. 2015. "Why biological water differs from $H2O$ and acts like a battery." In *Bioelectromagnetic and subtle energy medicine,* edited by Paul J. Rosch. Boca Raton, FL: Routledge/CRC Press.

Popp, Fritz-Albert. 2008. "Principles of complementary medicine in terms of a suggested scientific basis." *Indian Journal of Experimental Biology* 46 (5):378-383.

Potts, Wayne K. 1984. "The chorus-line hypothesis of manoeuvre coordination in avian flocks." *Nature* 309:344-345. doi: 10.1038/309344a0.

Pryor, Karen W. 1990. "Non-acoustic communication in small cetaceans: glance, touch, position, gesture, and bubbles." In *Sensory abilities of cetaceans: Laboratory and field evidence*, edited by Jeanette A. Thomas and Ronald A. Kastelein, 537-544. Berlin, Germany: Springer.

Radin, Dean I. 2006. *Entangled minds: Extrasensory experiences in a quantum reality.* New York, NY: Simon & Schuster.

Radin, Dean I., and Eva Lobach. 2007. "Toward understanding the placebo effect: Investigating a possible retrocausal factor." *Journal of Alternative & Complementary Medicine* 13 (7):733-740. doi: 10.1089/acm.2006.6243.

Radin, Dean I., and Roger D. Nelson. 1989. "Evidence for consciousness-related anomalies in random physical systems." *Foundations of Physics* 19 (12):1499-1514. doi: 10.1007/BF00732509.

Radin, Dean I., and M. J. Schlitz. 2005. "Gut feelings, intuition, and emotions: An exploratory study." *Journal of Alternative & Complementary Medicine* 11 (1):85-91. doi: 10.1089/acm.2005.11.85.

Ryan, Richard M., Netta Weinstein, Jessey Bernstein, Kirk Warren Brown, Louis Mistretta, and Marylène Gagné. 2010. "Vitalizing effects of being outdoors and in nature." *Journal of Environmental Psychology* 30 (2):159-168. doi: 10.1016/j.jenvp.2009.10.009.

Sahai, Ashok, and Raj Kumari Sahai. 2013. "Pineal gland: A structural and functional enigma." *Journal of the Anatomical Society of India* 62 (2):170-177. doi: 10.1016/j.jasi.2014.01.001.

Salvi, Carola, Emanuela Bricolo, John Kounios, Edward Bowden, and Mark Beeman. 2016. "Insight solutions are correct more often than analytic solutions." *Thinking & Reasoning* 22 (4):443-460. doi: 10.1080/13546783.2016.1141798.

Sato, Izuru, and Tamlin S. Conner. 2013. "The quality of time in nature: How fascination explains and enhances the relationship between nature experiences and daily affect." *Ecopsychology* 5 (3):197-204. doi: 10.1089/eco.2013.0026.

Savage-Rumbaugh, Sue, William Mintz Fields, and Jared Tagli-alatela. 2000. "Ape consciousness–human consciousness: A perspective informed by language and culture." *American Zoologist* 40 (6):910-921. doi: 10.1093/icb/40.6.910.

Schwartz, Stephen. 2014. "Through time and space: The evidence for remote viewing." In *The evidence for psi: The science of paranormal phenomena,* edited by D. Broderick and B. Groetzel, 332-426. Jefferson, NC: McFarland.

Snell, Tristan L., and Janette G. Simmonds. 2012. "Being in that environment can be very therapeutic": Spiritual experiences in nature." *Ecopsychology* 4 (4):326-335. doi: 10.1089/eco.2012.0078.

Strubbe, Bill. 2001. "A mind of its own." *Massage & Bodywork* 16 (2):44-49.

Sylvia, Claire, and William Novak. 1997. *A change of heart: A memoir.* Boston, MA: Little, Brown.

Talbot, Janet Frey, and Stephen Kaplan. 1986. "Perspectives on wilderness: Re-examining the value of extended wilderness experiences." *Journal of Environmental Psychology* 6 (3):177-188. doi: 10.1016/S0272-4944(86)80021-4.

Talbot, Michael. 1991. *The holographic universe.* New York, NY: Harper Collins.

Terasawa, Yuri, Yoshiya Moriguchi, Saiko Tochizawa, and Satoshi Umeda. 2014. "Interoceptive sensitivity predicts sensitivity to the emotions of others." *Cognition and Emotion* 28 (8):1435-1448. doi: 10.1080/02699931.2014.888988.

Troy, A. S., A. J. Shallcross, A. Brunner, R. Friedman, and M. C. Jones. 2018. "Cognitive reappraisal and acceptance: Effects on emotion, physiology, and perceived cognitive costs." *Emotion* 18 (1):58-74. doi: 10.1037/emo0000371.

Tsakiris, Manos. 2017. "The multisensory basis of the self: From body to identity to others." *The Quarterly Journal of Experimental Psychology* 70 (4):597-609. doi: 10.1080/17470218.2016.1181768.

Van Wijk, E. P., J. Ackerman, and R. Van Wijk. 2005. "Effect of meditation on ultraweak photon emission from hands and forehead." *Forsch Komplementarmed Klass Naturheilkd* 12 (2):107-112. doi: 10.1159/000084028.

Van Wijk, E. P., H. Koch, S. Bosman, and R. Van Wijk. 2006. "Anatomic characterization of human ultra-weak photon emission in practitioners of Transcendental Meditation(TM) and control subjects." *Journal of Alternative and Complementary Medicine* 12 (1):31-38. doi: 10.1089/acm.2006.12.31.

van Wijk, Eduard P. A., Roeland van Wijk, and Michal Cifra. 2007. "Spontaneous ultra-weak photon emission from human hands varies diurnally." European Conference on Biomedical Optics.

van Wijk, Roeland, Jan van der Greef, and Eduard P. A. van Wijk. 2010. "Human ultraweak photon emission and the Yin Yang concept of Chinese Medicine." *Journal of Acupuncture and Meridian Studies* 3 (4):221-231. doi: 10.1016/S2005-2901(10)60041-6.

Vigh, B, M. J. Manzano, Zádori A, CL Frank, A Lukáts, P Röhlich, Agoston Szél, and C. Dávid. 2002. "Nonvisual photoreceptors of the deep brain, pineal organs and retina." *Histology and Histopathology: Cellular and Molecular Biology* 17 (2):555-590. doi: 10.14670/HH-17.555.

Wilson, Edward O. 1984. *Biophilia.* Cambridge, MA: Harvard University Press.

Wohlleben, Peter. 2016. *The hidden life of trees: What they feel, how they communicate.* Translated by Jane Billinghurst. Vancouver, Canada: Greystone Books.

Wohlleben, Peter. 2017. *The inner life of animals: Love, grief, and compassion: Surprising observations of a hidden world.* Translated by Jane Billinghurst. Vancouver, Canada: Greystone Books.

Woiceshyn, Jaana. 2009. "Lessons from "Good Minds": How CEOs use intuition, analysis and guiding principles to make strategic decisions." *Long Range Planning* 42 (3):298-319. doi: 10.1016/j.lrp.2009.05.002.

ABOUT THE AUTHOR

Maura McCarley Torkildson is an author, speaker, artist, intuitive and Soul Creativity Support Mentor. She is the founder of Maura Torkildson Coaching and her work includes supporting creatives and spiritual women entrepreneurs to complete their creative soul projects. She is a Certified Professional Co-Active Coach and has an M.A. in Women's Spirituality from New College of California. Her artwork has been exhibited in both the U.S. and Malta.

www.MauraTorkildsonCoaching.com

About the Foreword Author: **Randy Fauver, Ph.D.,** is a professor of integrative medicine and psychology at the California Institute of Integral Studies, John F. Kennedy University, and the California Institute for Human Science. He is a Research Fellow with the BIAL Foundation, leading research into mind-body interactions at the California Institute of Integral Studies. He has degrees and certifications from Bastyr University, the Institute of Transpersonal Psychology, Harvard University, and Stanford University, where he did NIH-funded research in the School of Medicine and was founding director of the Integral Health research and education program. He spent several years apprenticing with the spiritual leader of a Native American community in Colorado.

Thank you for reading *The Inner Tree*. Please pass the torch of connection by helping other readers find this book. Here are some suggestions for your consideration:

- Write an online customer review wherever books are sold

- Gift this book to family and friends

- Share a photo of yourself with the book on social media and tag #TheInnerTree and #MauraMcCarleyTorkildson

- Bring in Maura as a speaker for your club or organization

- Suggest *The Inner Tree* to your local book club, and download the *Book Club Discussion Questions* from www.CitrinePublishing.com/bookclubs

- For group orders of ten books or more, contact Citrine Publishing at (828) 585-7030 or Publisher@CitrinePublishing.com

- Connect with the author online by visiting www.MauraTorkildsonCoaching.com

Made in the USA
San Bernardino, CA
13 October 2018